A PRISONER'S CRY

Look Up, Your Redemption Draws Near!

Johnny Paul Collins, B.Th

ISBN 979-8-88832-091-4 (paperback)
ISBN 979-8-88832-092-1 (digital)

Christian Faith Publishing
832 Park Avenue
Meadville, PA 16335
www.christianfaithpublishing.com

Printed in the United States of America

IT IS DONE

From heaven to earth,
No distance too far.
You stepped down from your thrown,
To open the door.

With love in your eyes,
They drove nails through your hands.
And determined to die,
You passed no judgment on them.

You say no sin is too great,
But I felt the cost was too high.
That the King of all glory,
Should lay down His life.

So here, Lord, I kneel,
With tears streaming down.
Confessing my sins,
Ashamed how they sound.

But now lifting me up,
You wipe each tear one by one,
And smiling in love,
You say, "What's done is now done."

By Johnny Paul Collins
Ironwood State Prison
September 20, 2020

PREFACE

As a youth, I recall being told a story of a Christian man who had built his home on the side of a mountain that turned out to be an active volcano. One day, a geologist drove up the mountain road leading to his home to warn him that scientific readings revealed that the volcano was about to erupt and advised the Christian man that he needed to collect his things and flee to safety because he would not survive the eruption. The Christian man explained to the geologist, in protest, that he was a man of faith, that God would protect him, and that, if God was about to cause the volcano to erupt, then He would have made that plan known to the Christian mountaineer.

Deeply troubled by the Christian's hardheadedness and refusal to leave, the geologist drove straight to the ranger station to request that a ranger drive up to the cabin and press the man to leave. A ranger was dispatched to the mountain cabin to try and talk some sense into the Christian mountaineer and get him to flee to safety, but the man refused to leave his home and repeated the same beliefs and position to the ranger that he had shared with the geologist.

Finally, a close and trusted friend of the Christian mountaineer heard of the impending doom and drove up to beg his friend to leave, but still, the Christian man refused to do so. That night the volcano erupted and a huge blanket of lava rushed down the mountain side killing the Christian man before he could escape. Standing before the thrown of God, the perplexed man asked Jesus why He did not reveal the event to him and protect him from being killed by the river of molten lava, to which Jesus replied, "I sent three people who warned you that the volcano was about to erupt and told you to flee, but you refused to listen."

The purpose and intent of this book is to inform my Christian brothers and sisters that global events are occurring, which signal the start of a prophetic season and to warn nonbelievers to flee to the safety of the Cross of Christ before the tragedies that are now coming upon the earth overtakes them. For those among us who have been paying attention to the global catastrophes, hostilities, and suffering, and who know the prophetic significance of them, there is no doubt that we are seeing the Beginning of Sorrows and that our redemption is drawing near. Just as with the messengers sent to the Christian mountaineer in the story, I cannot force any to heed my warning and flee to Jesus for safety, but nonetheless, I feel compelled to sound the alarm. Alas, I am only a messenger.

ACKNOWLEDGMENTS

FOREMOST, THIS BOOK is dedicated to my Lord and Savior, Jesus Christ, and God our Father, who, through the Holy Spirit, inspired me to share the insights that were being revealed to me, during my in-depth studies of End-Times prophecies, to the glory and honor of He who sits on the throne over heaven and earth. Father, it is by Your will that I exist and live, and so all that I am I place at Your feet in thankful reverence.

Secondly, I dedicate this book to my beautiful wife, Eileen Marie Collins, who was sent to me by God, and who has stood by my side loving and supporting me on my best of days, and when things have not been so great. Thank you, "Little Tyka," for being the woman of faith that I asked God to send to me and the best friend that I had hoped to find and spend the rest of my life with. I love and appreciate you more than I know how to express in words.

And thirdly, this book is dedicated to those many loving and supportive family members who have refused to forget about me in spite of my current situation, which include the following: Virginia Standridge (my mother), Karyn Kyle (my spiritual mother), Jack Kyle (my spiritual father), Karen Degolyer (my spiritual daughter), Pedro Valdes (my stepson), Catherine Collins (my daughter), Gwendolyn Collins (my daughter), Ashley [Collins] (my daughter), John Degolyer (my spiritual son), Johnny Collins II (my son), Alex Wisdom (my grandson), Adrian Wisdom (my granddaughter), Kyle [Collins] (my grandson), Johnny Collins III (my grandson), Sophia Degolyer (my spiritual granddaughter), Brier [Collins] (my granddaughter), Joey Collins (my brother), Denise Collins (my sister) Scarlet [Collins] (my granddaughter), and David Standridge (my brother). Thank you all for giving me the love and support that each of you does in your own special way.

The Beginning-of-Sorrows Prophecy

Then Jesus went out and departed from the temple, and His disciples came up to show Him the buildings of the temple. And Jesus said to them, "Do you not see all these things? Assuredly, I say to you, not one stone shall be left here upon another, that shall not be thrown down."

Now as He sat on the Mount of Olives, the disciples came to Him privately, saying, "Tell us, when will these things be? And what will be the sign of Your coming, and of the end of the age?"

And Jesus answered and said to them: "Take heed that no one deceives you. For many will come in My name, saying, 'I am the Christ,' and will deceive many. And you will hear of wars and rumors of wars. See that you are not troubled; for all these things must come to pass, but the end is not yet. For nation will rise against nation, and kingdom against kingdom. And there will be famines, pestilences, and earthquakes in various places. All these are the beginning of sorrows." (Matthew 24:1–8)

CHAPTER 1

The Signs of the Time
Introduction: the Questions

- Are we fast approaching the "end of the age" and the "Second Coming" of Jesus Christ as was foretold in the Bible?
- Are there real and present *signs* taking place which confirm that we are witnessing the "Beginning of Sorrows"?
- Are we the *generation that will not pass away* before the *Second Coming* of Jesus?
- Is it possible for us to know and understand the signs that reveal the prophetic *season* that we are now in?
- What should we be doing as believers if the answer to these questions is *yes*?

BEING BORN AND—PRIMARILY—RAISED in the *Bible Belt* of the United States (i.e., rural Arkansas) by God-fearing evangelical Christian parents, I had often heard from the adults in my youth that, "The end of the world is coming soon," and that "Jesus could return at any time." These kinds of jolting exclamations were usually uttered after a local or national news broadcaster had reported that some *wacko* in the world (such as David Koresh out in Waco, Texas, in the early 1990s) was discovered claiming to be Jesus reincarnate, that a recent war would be erupting, that there would be food shortages in some third-world country (such as Africa), that there would be an outbreak of a newly discovered disease (such as HIV and AIDS in the early 1980s), or that there would be a devastating earthquake. Later in life, I would come to realize that the adults who had exclaimed such warnings following those aforementioned events had not done so with the intent to mislead me or anyone else who may have heard them, but rather, they had simply misunderstood a specific set, or cluster, of End-Times prophecies which Jesus himself provided for us in Matthew 24:3–14 as signs that we are instructed to look for, so that we as believers could know the season of the end of the age and His Second Coming.

In Matthew 24:3–14, the Bible tells us that, as Jesus sat on the Mount of Olives, His disciples came to Him privately asking three specific questions. The disciples wanted to know (1) when the buildings of the temple which Jesus had referred to earlier in this same chapter be would "thrown down"; (2) what the *sign* of His [second] coming would be; and (3) what the *sign* of the end of the age would be. This book focuses on questions 2 and 3.

Jesus does go on to answer them, but since it is evident that none of the disciples of which Jesus was speaking in this instance are still physically alive today, we can then logically conclude that when Jesus responded to their questions and stated that *you* will see and hear and experience all these *signs* and consequences, that He meant the Christian believers that are alive and on the earth at the time which God has appointed for all these events to happen.

With the above conclusion resolved—for those of us who have sought to understand the scripture—we read how Jesus goes on to explain to the disciples, and to us, that there are a *cluster* of specific *signs* that will take place, which believers should watch out for to know for certain that we are in the *season* of the End Times and Jesus's Second Coming. These *signs* consist of (1) many impostors of Jesus coming forward who are successful in deceiving many believers, (2) wars and rumors of wars, (3) an escalation in tensions between nations, (4) an escalation in tensions between kingdoms, (5) famines, (6) pestilences, and (7) earthquakes, in various places.

After these signs or "Beginning of Sorrows" as the Word of God reads in Matthew 24:8, Jesus tells us that we—as the Christian body—will suffer tribulation and be killed for our faith and that we will be hated by all nations for His name's sake. Many false prophets will rise up at this appointed time in history and will deceive many, and, because lawlessness will abound, the love of many people on the earth will grow cold. Jesus says to the Christian believers who go through these harsh and trying End-Times events that, if they endure to the end, they will be saved. As a final marker, Jesus explained that the preaching of the gospel of the kingdom will take place throughout the world as a witness to all the nations, and then the end will come (Matthew 24:14).

In defense of my parents and the other adults of my youth who had vigilantly—albeit erroneously—sounded alarms that "the end of the age" and Jesus's "Second Coming" to the earth was at hand, it is historically accurate to take note of the fact that we have seen most, if not all, of the *kinds* of events that Jesus told us would occur, taking place at varying locations and at differing periods in history around the world, since He physically ascended to heaven to be seated at the right hand of the Father.

Indeed, over the past two thousand years or so, mankind has recorded numerous instances of Jesus's impostors rising up, wars and rumors of wars, civil and national unrest, famines, diseases, and earthquakes, in various places—all without Jesus returning.

Ironically, these kinds of historical events taking place, with "the end of the age" and the "Second Coming" of Jesus not occurring, seemingly serve to lend evidentiary support to the ungodly proposition that the Bible and its End-Times prophecies are nothing more than ancient myths and fictional stories that were designed to keep the human populations of the earth under control, among those who know, and yet reject, the Word of God.

Admittedly, I myself had come to question the truthfulness and accuracy of the Bible and its prophecies in my youth, for a time, because of the events discussed above taking place, the alarms of the adults sounding, and yet Jesus never showing up.

It was only later in my mid-twenties that I started to re-evaluate these scriptures of End-Times prophecies, and what Jesus had literally said, for myself, that I realized why so many had misunderstood the future *signs* and *seasons* that Jesus had spoken about and told us to watch for.

The Lord revealed to me through His Spirit that all seven *signs* mentioned in Matthew 24:5–8 must be taking place at the same time, and on a global scale, for them to mark the start of the period in prophecy that Jesus had referred to as the Beginning of Sorrows and not just the occurrence of the first, or the last event, taking place independently of all the others and separated by time, as many have thought and preached in times past.

Stated a different way, these prophetic *signs* that mark the Beginning of Sorrows and the start of the End Times will come in a cluster of global events that are visibly taking place at the same time, as opposed to one occurring for instance in 1991, then another in 2001, and another in 2021, and so on. However, the seven events do not have to necessarily have the same start dates, biblically speaking. For example, the "wars and rumors of wars" do not have to begin at the same time (date and moment) as the "famines" and "pestilences" and "earthquakes" in various places—*signs*, it is only essential to the prophecy that all the seven events be taking place, at some point, at the same time and on a global scale (i.e., not just in one or two places). If one of the seven events—or *signs*—is not occurring, then we can know for certain that the Beginning of Sorrows that Jesus spoke of in His prophecy has not yet started.

It is my understanding and belief that the Christian *body* members who are present on the earth and who are witnesses to these first seven *signs* foretold by Jesus in Matthew 24:5–8, occurring, will not be present for the beginning of the coming tribulations that are also explained by our Lord in verses 9 through 14. That is to say, I believe that the church, as already constituted at the occurrence of the first seven *signs*, will be raptured somewhere around the time that all seven events are taking place, but before the *global* hardships, *global* murders, and *global* Christian hatred ensues, which Jesus prophesied about in verses nine through fourteen. Moreover, I believe that the

Christian brothers and sisters who will be subjected to those tribulations outlined in verses nine through fourteen, who are killed and hated on a global scale by all nations, will be those that convert to Christianity at some point after the rapture of the current believers from the earth. These new converts will be the ones who will complete the mission of preaching the gospel of the kingdom of God to all the world as a witness to all nations, and thus, usher at the end of the age. Simply stated, I believe that the simultaneous occurrence of all seven *signs* discussed in this book, preludes the rapture of the Church and the beginning of the tribulation period for the earth and those who continue to dwell on it after we are gone.

In this book, we will evaluate the seven signs a bit closer and compare them to modern-day global events of which I propose parallels and fulfills Jesus's prophecies regarding the Beginning of Sorrows. Jesus tells us in Matthew 24 that we will see, hear, and experience these seven *signs*, as the Christian Church, on a global scale. So are we at a point in biblical prophecy where we are able to witness the events that Jesus told us that we would be when the end of the age is nearing, and He is preparing to return? I am of the opinion that we are, and I now humbly invite you to journey along with me through the pages of this book, to determine the answer to that question for yourself. However, before we get started, it is important that I emphatically express that I am by no means suggesting to you that we can learn *the day* or *the hour* on which the end of the age will occur or when Jesus will return to the earth to set up His kingdom. I only submit to you that we can identify the prophetic *starting point* leading up to those events, just as Jesus instructed us that we could in the book of Matthew 24:32–36.

> Now learn this parable from the fig tree: When its branch has already become tender and puts forth leaves, you know that summer is near. So you also, when you see all these things, know that it is near—at the doors! Assuredly, I say to you, this generation will by no means pass away till all these things take place. Heaven and earth will

pass away, but My words will by no means pass away. But of the day and hour no one knows, not even the angels of heaven, but My Father only.

(Scripture taken from the New King James Version®. © 1982, by Thomas Nelson. Used by permission. All rights reserved)

CHAPTER 2

Jesus's Impostors

Now as He sat on the Mount of Olives, the Disciples came to
Him privately, saying, "Tell us, when will these things be? And
what will be the sign of your coming, and of the end of the age?"
And Jesus answered and said to them: "Take heed that
no one deceives you. For many will come in my name,
saying, 'I am the Christ,' and will deceive many."

—Matthew 24:3–5

BEFORE WE CAN accurately examine this portion of Jesus's *End-Times* prophecy, it seems necessary for us to revisit the earlier conclusion that I had advanced regarding the issue of who Jesus was speaking to when He stated that *you* will see, and hear, and experience all these signs. There is much logic and support for the conclusion that Jesus was speaking to a future generation of Christian believers in the passage. First, as I said earlier, all the disciples whom Jesus was with in this particular instance were no longer physically alive on the face of the earth. Second, there would have been no realistic way that the disciples (or other Christian believers who were living in that day and age) could have been witnesses to global events such as what Jesus was explaining because the Christian movement had not yet expanded globally, and even if it had, Jesus inferred that all the hearers of His prophecy, living at "the occurrent time in human history, would see and hear and experience the events." And third, Jesus specifically stated that the *generation* who would begin witnessing all these events, in the appointed time, will *not pass away* (i.e., die off) before the prophecy is completed (Matthew 24:34.)

In light of Jesus's statement regarding a future *generation* of believers who are alive on the face of the earth at that point in time—a time beyond that of the twelve disciples—and who will then become eyewitnesses to the unfolding seven prophetic events that will commence the Beginning of Sorrows and illuminate the start of the tribulation period, which occurs immediately after the rapture of the Christian believers who are on the earth at that time, it then becomes important for us to take a look at the generations of people who are alive in our lifetime and decide whether or not any could be *the generation* whom Jesus declared would witness all these things and who would *not pass away* before the prophecy is fulfilled.

It seems prudent to me to lay a definitional foundation for the word *generation* before we get started with our examination of the generations of people who are alive on the earth today. The *Concise Oxford English Dictionary: 11ᵗʰ Ed. Revised © Oxford University Press 2008* defines the word *generation* as: "all the people born and living at about the same time, regarded collectively; the average period in which children grow up and have children of their own (usually reckoned as about thirty years.)" So for example, a group of people all born between 1900 and 1910 and reaching the age of thirty between 1930 and 1940 would all be classified as the same generation. For our examination of the prophetic *generation,* it is critical that we remember that generational adulthood and individual adulthood are defined in a much different way. Generational adulthood is reached at about thirty years, and individual adulthood is generally set under laws at eighteen years. Here, our examination(s) relies only on generational adulthood calculations.

There are currently four individual generations of people who are living on the face of the earth today. Those being, the baby boomers, Generation X, millennials, and Generation Z. Are one of these four generations *the generation* that will fulfill Jesus's prophecy of witnessing the Beginning of Sorrows, the tribulation period, and His Second Coming, without *passing away*? I believe that one is, and so, let us closely examine each of these together for me to demonstrate to you why I have reached that sure conclusion.

- Baby boomers—The baby boomers are the generation of people born after World War II (that is between 1945 and 1955) and who are currently between the ages of 65 and 75 years old.
- Generation X—Generation X is the generation of people born after the baby boomers (between the mid-1960s and the mid-1970s) and who are currently between the ages of 45 and 55 years old.
- Millennials—Millennials are the generation of people born in the mid-1980s through the mid-1990s who are between 25 and 35 years old.
- Generation Z—Generation Z is the generation of children and young adults now alive on the earth who were born between the years 2000 and 2010 and who currently range in age from 12 to 22 years old. By the year 2030, these young people will reach the point of generational adulthood. (It is important to note that the children who may have already been born to the young people of Generation Z and those who could be born over the next eight years are not yet a formally recognized generation with regard to them being given an official title or name for their generation.)

To the extent that there is a five-year time gap between the generations listed, a person born between two generations in that five-year period would relate themselves to the generation that is nearest to their own age group by years, months, and even by days if necessary to reach a determinative membership. Admittedly, the system used to make these categorical determinations is man-made and therefore far from perfect. Nonetheless, it is our reference point for the task at hand (i.e., in distinguishing generations) and is accurate enough to be used for such.

Now that we have identified the four relevant generations on the earth today, we must turn our attention to determining which of the four fit into the framework of Jesus's prophecy and discuss how and why we are able to make such a determination if indeed we can.

Looking at Jesus's prophecies from a modern-day and realistic perspective, there is no way that every Christian believer who is on the face of the earth could be a simultaneous witness of those events, which He told all of us to watch for without the advent and use of our current day technologies. That is to say, in today's world, we are able to turn on a radio, television, computer, or even a cell phone and become witnesses to events such as wars and famines and earthquakes taking place all around the globe at the same time, without us being physically present for any of them.

I have no doubt that Jesus had all these modern-day technological advancements in mind and was speaking specifically about one of the four generations alive on the earth today when He said that *you* will see and hear and experience all these events at the Beginning of Sorrows. Based on this logical analysis, it then becomes necessary for us to look at each of these four information gateways (i.e., radio, television, computers, and cell phones) to consider their informative value and accessibility to those of us who Jesus said would be the Beginning of Sorrows—witnesses of that day.

- Radio—In the mid-1890s, Guglielmo Marconi developed the first apparatus for transmitting long-distance radio communication. On December 23, 1900, a Canadian inventor by the name of Reginald A. Fessenden became the first person to send an audio transmission by means of electromagnetic waves, successfully transmitting over a distance of about a mile. Six years later, on December 24, 1906, Mr. Fessenden became the first person to make a public broadcast over the radio. By the mid-1930s, radio technology was being used for news broadcasts and entertainment purposes in many homes and businesses across the face of our world, and today most people in the world have access to such a device. Although the creation of radio technology eventually became useful for the distribution of local and national news broadcasts and entertainment in its early primitive state (i.e., as a *radio* device), it has never been widely used for the distribution of international news broadcasts and information sharing for humanity at large. That is to say, the information that we have access to from traditional radio use is that which is germane to our city, county, state, or nation but is almost never relating events occurring in different nations around the world. Therefore, one would find it to be near impossible to keep up with globally occurring prophetic events if they could only rely on the use of primitive radio technology as an exclusive source of information, but it has some limited use.

- Television—Electronic television was first successfully demonstrated in San Francisco, California, on September 7, 1927. The system was designed by Philo Taylor Farnsworth, who was only twenty-one years old at the time and who had himself grown up in a home without the luxury of electricity until he turned fourteen. There are few inventions that have had as much effect on global society as the television has. This is especially true when related to the time before the invention and promulgation of the Internet as it exists today. Before 1947, the number of US homes containing television sets numbered in the thousands, but by the late 1990s, around 98 percent of U.S. families had at least one television set at home and that was being watched around seven hours a day; my home included among them.

  In today's world, television devices in human dwellings are as commonplace as a *kitchen range and running water*; that is to say, they are nearly universally present. Despite the fact that the personal ownership of television technology is measured on a global scale and is thought to allow us the opportunity to see and hear local, national, and world events as they happen(ed), the content (i.e., news and relative information) that is distributed by the public and private television network broadcasters is often anything but holistic and unbiased. In recent years, the phrase "fake news" has been coined to remind us of this very fact. As a consequence, even though it is possible for television technology to provide some measure of factual insight into prophetic—global—events that are taking place, oftentimes the information being aired is purposefully fragmented and presented in such a way that it distorts or conceals the full truth. For example, the nation of China used its government-owned and operated television outlets to conceal the truth about the origin and infection rate of COVID-19 in early 2020 from its population and the rest of the world; a cover-up that continues. Another example might be the information that had been distributed by US news broadcasting networks, which are owned and operated by members of the Democratic Party, who had actively worked to prevent the re-election of Donald J. Trump, by painting him as a *racist* and a *bigot* to American voters. The power that these news broadcasters wield over the unwitting viewer is nothing less than frightening and will no doubt be exploited by the soon-materializing Antichrist during the tribulation period that is fast approaching; I digress. The point is that television technology is useful to aid Christian believers who are deliberate and watchful—on a global scale—for all the prophetic events that Jesus instructed believers to look for and has been available to us on a global scale since the 1990s, but we must use discernment.

- Computers—The first personal computer (PC) was introduced in 1975, the MITS ALTAIR 8800. In 1976, the world was introduced to the first word-processing program for PCs. Then in 1981, a company named IBM unveiled its PC, the IBM 5150, followed by Apple's new MACINTOSH PC in 1984. By 2002, the total number of PCs, including desktop and laptop machines of all types, shipped from scores of manufacturers since 1975, reached one billion. In 2010, Apple released its iPad tablet computer and sold more than three million devices in the first eighty days. By year-end 2016, according to the *Computer Industry Almanac*, the US had 380.2 million PCs in use.

Despite the staggering number of PCs sold, private citizens who owned them across the face of the planet did not have access to the global Internet (i.e., a link to humanity at large) until the mid- to late-1990s. Notably, in 2008 a company named Google® introduced its "Chrome" browser (a program with an interface for displaying HTML files, used to navigate the World Wide Web), which greatly widened Internet research. By 2012, Chrome ranked as the most widely used browser in the world, according to StatCounter.com. By 2014, the number of Internet websites passed one billion, and by year-end of 2016, global Internet traffic surpassed one zettabyte (one trillion gigabytes), according to networking giant Cisco. It is indisputable that since the mid- to late-1990s to the present, computer Internet access offers its users more effective research tools for collecting information on global prophetic events than any other technology at the watchful Christian believer's disposal. Technological advancements in the Internet in recent years, such as hand-held video and live-streaming broadcasting capabilities, provide humanity at large with an opportunity to see and hear and experience global events as they are unfolding in one location, from any other location on the face of the earth, an invaluable resource for our global observation and research.

- Cell phone—In 1962 NASA launched the world's first active communications satellite, AT&T's Telstar 1. Although cell phones became available on the public market in the years that followed, it was not until 1994 that the first *smartphone* (a mobile phone which incorporates a palmtop computer), that being IBM's Simon Personal Communicator, came to the public market. The device was state of the art with such features as an address book, calendar, email capability, and an assortment of games. In

August 1996, a company named Nokia released its Nokia 9000 Communicator, which contained all those features included in IBM's device, but which offered text-based Web browsing as well. Then in June 1999, Qualcomm released its pdQ Smartphone, which provided the user with an integrated palm PDA and Internet connectivity. In 2007, Apple released its iPhone, beginning an era of multifunctional high-tech smartphones. By year-end 2012, more than one billion smartphones of all types were in use worldwide. Today, nearly every person on the face of the planet has a cell phone themselves or access to the use one. With Internet capability, these modern-day mini hand-held computers provide the user with nearly the same research tools as that a home-PC user.

There is no doubt that Jesus had all these technological advancements in mind when He instructed the future generations of Christian believers to watch for all these signs in the season to come. If not, it is difficult to understand how every single Christian believer on the face of the earth, who was watching for the events, could possibly see and hear and experience all the global events, *simultaneously*, and thereby, know the prophesied season was at hand in its appointed time. Truly, the technologies of which are at our current disposal (i.e., radios, televisions, computer Internet, and cell phone Internet) can facilitate every Christian brother and sister on the face of the earth witnessing the prophetic global events, simultaneously, and I believe that Jesus intended that we employ them to do exactly that.

As we continue to move through the pages of this book together, I will provide evidence (which you can research and separately verify) to prove that all seven prophetic events that Jesus told us to watch for, and that mark the Beginning of Sorrows, are now occurring on the global stage. The fact that all seven events are happening at the same time, on a global scale, and that Christian believers who know the prophecy have an opportunity—through those technologies identified—to be simultaneous witnesses to the *signs* and thereby identify the *season* should be a cause for celebration for those of us who have placed our hope in Jesus.

Now to provide you with the answer to the question of who I believe the *generation* of believers are whom Jesus prophesied would certainly *not pass away* before the end of the age and His Second Coming. In identifying this *generation*, it was necessary for me to find out which of the four generations were alive at the time that all four categories of technology became available; who had reached young adulthood (because I do not believe that Jesus was intending for children to watch out for and identify the seven signs); and who have had the ability to be witnesses to all seven global events taking place on a global scale through technological advancements.

The mission of identifying that generation who has satisfied all three of these requirements left me with the feeling of being on a childhood treasure hunt, knowing that if they were among us, it would not be long before we were with our Redeemer in heaven and enjoying all the treasures which we have *stored up* there while serving Him down here, including the real treasure of being in His presence.

Now imagine my surprise and excitement when I realized that, just like in every children's treasure-hunt story, *X* marked the spot—Generation X. It was Generation X who was the first generation—globally speaking—to start seeing and hearing and experiencing the prophetic events taking place, in the mid- to late-1990s, through the proliferation of television and Internet-connected devices and who continued to witness them now, through advances in technologies in the twenty-first century, and there is no other generation evaluated that satisfies these requirements.

Today, much of the baby boomers generation is passing away in record numbers; the millennials' generation was too young to read and understand the Bible's prophecies and to watch for them in the mid-1990s, and Generation Z was not born yet. Taking into account the fact that all the prophetic events are occurring now, it is Generation X that satisfies Jesus's description of the generation who would start to witness these events on a global scale and who would *not pass away* until the end of the age came and He returns as King of kings and Lord of lords.

Moving forward, in the first of the seven *signs* Jesus tells us that when the prophetic End-Times season is upon us, we will see many Jesus's impostors rising to public recognition and that these impostors will be effective in deceiving many. So to begin our journey into the prophetic events that Jesus told us that we should pay attention to, we must investigate whether or not there are *many* Jesus's impostors currently living among us on the earth who have made their blasphemous claims of being Jesus reincarnated known to humanity at large. Moreover, because Jesus implied that this information will be available to the generation of Christian believers who are instructed to watch for the prophetic events, we need to take a look at how accessible the information is if in fact there are folks out there in the world now professing to be our Lord.

First, we will look at whether or not such information is able to be readily ascertained by believers who are looking for it in earnest. I would submit to you that the information needs to be available to the public on a *global scale* to satisfy the underlying intent and parameter of the prophetic *sign*, just as well as the information relating to the *other six* remaining *signs* needs to be.

Turning to the ease and availability of modern-day technology, this task is easily accomplished by anyone with a computer or cell phone having Internet access, by simply Googling® a search for "List of People Who Claimed to be Jesus." In so doing, it will become quite evident that there are several websites that have—and manage—a list of persons from the past and some who are currently living who have been labeled by others and who claim themselves to be Jesus—one of which being Wikipedia®.

There are many that scoff at Wikipedia® and question the value and accuracy of the information found there, but I believe that it is an excellent resource for information and research because it was created by the people, for the people, and the governments of the world do not have a hand in the information being distributed by it. Moreover, the list made globally accessible on Wikipedia® covers a vast period of time in history starting in the eighteenth century and provides a list of names of Jesus's impostors spanning up until our present time; the list revealing the names of forty-three Jesus's impostors in all. I have duplicated the names along with other information that I had thought to be relevant to achieve a full understanding, below:

Eighteenth century
- Kondratiy Selivanov (c. 1730s–1832). Russia
- Ann Lee (1736–1784). Location unknown.

Nineteenth century
- John Nichols Thom (1799–1838). England
- Arnold Potter (1813–1880). Location unknown
- Baha'u'llah (1817–1892). Location unknown
- William W. Davies (1833–1906). Walla Walla, Washington, USA
- Mirza Ghulam Ahmad of Qadian/Indian (1835–1908). India

Twentieth century
- John Hugh Smyth-Pigott (1852–1927). Location unknown
- Haile Selassie I (1892–1975). Jamaica
- Lou de Palingboer (1898–1968). The Netherlands
- Ernest Norman (1904–1971). USA
- Krishna Venta (1911–1958). San Francisco, California USA.
- Ahn Sahng-hong (1918–1985). South Korea
- Sun Myung Moon (1920–2012). Location unknown
- Clyde Benson (lifespan unknown). Location unknown
- Joseph Cassel (lifespan unknown). Location unknown
- Leon Gabor (lifespan unknown). Location unknown
- Jim Jones (1931–1978). Jonestown, Guyana, South America
- Marshall Applewhite (1931–1997). USA
- Charles Manson (1934–2017). Southern California, USA
- Yahweh ben Yahweh (1935–2007). Liberty City, Florida, USA
- Laszlo Toth (1938–2012). Australia
- Wayne Bent (1941–). Location unknown
- Ariffin Mohammed (1943–2016). Location unknown.
- Mitsuo Matayoshi (1944–2018). Japan
- Tony Quinn (1944–). Ireland

- José Luis de Jesus Miranda (1946–2013). Miami, Florida, USA
- Inri Cristo (1948–). Brazil, South America
- Thomas Harrison Provenzano (1949–2000). USA
- Shoko Asahara (1955–2018). Japan
- David Koresh (1959–1993). Waco, Texas, USA
- Hogen Fukunaga (1945–). Japan
- Marina Tsvigun (1960–). Location unknown
- Sergey Torop (1961–). Southern Siberia, Russia
- Douglas Metcalf (1921–1968). North Canterbury, New Zealand
- Stuart Walker (1957–). Sydney, Australia
- GG Allin (1956–1993). Location unknown

Twenty-first century
- Apollo Quiboloy (1950–). The Philippines
- Hasan Mezarci (1954–). The Republic of Turkey
- Alan John Miller (1962–). Australia
- David Shayler (1965–). Great Britain
- Maurice Clemmons (1972–2009). Washington State, USA
- Oscar Ramiro Ortega-Hernandez (1990–). Washington D.C., USA

This list is anything but exhaustive with regard to the total number of people who have, and that is currently, claiming to be Jesus incarnate. What this list represents are those who have been successful in commanding the world's attention as a result of their treacherous claim and ability to persuade thousands, if not hundreds of thousands or even millions, collectively, that they are in fact the Second Coming of our Lord Jesus. At the end of the list that I have referenced above, Wikipedia® suggests website visitors conduct additional inquiries by using the search terms:

- Cult of personality
- Doomsday cult
- Jerusalem syndrome

- Jewish Messiah claimants
- List of avatar claimants
- List of Buddha claimants
- List of founders of religious traditions
- List of Mahdi claimants
- List of Messiah claimants
- List of people who have been considered deities
- Messiah
- Messiah complex
- Messianism
- Religious delusion
- Unfulfilled Christian religious predictions
- Hong Xiuquan, claimed to be Jesus's little brother

Admittedly, some of the terms referenced above do not seem to be directly related to individuals claiming to be Jesus reincarnated, and I did not personally venture to obtain information related to these additional terms because I felt that the search term that I have relied on was more directly on point. With that said, I am sure that conducting research into these additional terms would have yielded the names of additional individuals claiming to be the *Messiah*, or *Savior*, or *Son of God*, or *God*, and the like. Ergo, I encourage the reader to conduct your own Internet inquiries into these search terms if you require more evidence of the fulfillment of the prophecy, or you are interested in assembling a more exhaustive list beyond that which I have provided.

So now we must determine whether or not the public information which we have looked at and considered satisfies the prophetic *sign* of *many* coming in Jesus's name claiming that they are the Christ, who have been, and are, successful in deceiving *many*. To do so, we need to clarify what the definition of the word *many* is. The word is defined by the *Concise Oxford English Dictionary: 11th Edition Revised © Oxford University Press 2008* as "a large number." In reviewing the Wikipedia® list of individuals claiming to be Jesus, we can conclude that forty-three men and women have been called Jesus by others or have personally claimed to be Him. Out of these forty-three Jesus impostors, as many as twelve are still alive on the face of the earth today. There is a real possibility that there are many more currently living; however, it is difficult to give an exact number given my restrained search.

To put all this into perspective, if a well-known and loved religious leader died today (like Billy Graham whom we just lost a couple of years ago), how many people do you honestly think would show up centuries after their death and undertake the mission of trying to convince large gatherings of people, and even all the human race if possible, that they are in fact the reincarnation of the person that had passed away? The common-sense answer to that question would be "none," right? Correct. So forty-three false Jesus claimants showing up just over the past four centuries, of which *at least twelve* are still living, is a relatively large number of people which can accurately be described as many, right?

Another interesting fact that we should take notice of is that all twelve currently living Jesus's impostors are well-spread-out and occupy nearly every continent on the face of the earth: North and South America, Europe, Asia, Africa, and Australia. Indeed, Satan and his false messengers are working overtime to spread deception to the ends of the earth as quickly as they can because they know our Lord is coming back soon, and that their time is short.

Consequently, these Jesus impostors have been very successful in deceiving thousands, if not hundreds of thousands or maybe even millions of people searching for the true Jesus. Indeed, a few, namely Jim Jones, Marshall Applewhite, and David Koresh, were even able to convince their followers to commit suicide in mass, as a way to usher at the end of the age or for some other ridiculous or sadistic reason. The level of influence that these false Christs had, and do possess, over their followers is mind-boggling to me.

To convince even a single person to listen to you is often a task that is unachievable in today's world, so to command such control and influence that these Jesus's impostors are over the masses, given their selling point, is almost supernatural in my opinion. Making a comparison, at the time that I was writing this page of the book, the world was twenty months into the global COVID-19 pandemic, and those world leaders who are in government positions and ruling over the populations of the earth were finding it extremely hard to influence their populations to take necessary steps to avoid contracting the disease and dying, something as simple as wearing a face mask if they do venture out of their homes, without force.

David Koresh and these other Jesus's impostors are able to convince their followers to kill themselves without a second thought. So the level of sway that these Jesus's impostors are wielding is uniquely frightening and can be nothing less than demonically energized. Surely it was this kind of influence that Jesus had wanted us to be on guard against and watch for in Matthew 24:4–5.

In light of the foregoing, I believe that there is more than enough factual and convincing evidence to support the conclusion that the first of the seven prophetic *signs* which Jesus told us to watch for is occurring in our generation (i.e., "Generation X"). There can be no serious objection to the position that many have come in Jesus's name claiming to be the Christ and have deceived many; therefore, this part of the prophecy is satisfied.

FALSE CHRISTS

CHAPTER 3

Global Warfare

And you will hear of wars and rumors of wars.
See that you are not troubled; for all these things
must come to pass, but the end is not yet.
—Matthew 24:6

SINCE AS FAR back as world history books have recorded, there have been wars and rumors of wars occurring between nations and peoples from every kindred, across the face of the entire earth, and this was no less true in the time that our Lord Jesus walked the earth. So reading this *sign* and determining its uniqueness or corresponding relevance to the *season* of the end of the age and the Second Coming of Jesus requires a more focused study of the Bible prophecy, itself, and of the specific words Christ used.

First, and probably most important in my opinion, Jesus tells us—as the Christian believers who are alive on the face of the earth at the Beginning of Sorrows—that we will "hear of wars and rumors of wars" as opposed to seeing or participating in the wars ourselves, when this prophetic *sign*, which helps to reveal the prophetic season, is occurring. Second, Jesus tells us not to be *troubled* when these wars and rumors of wars are taking place at this specific point in time. And third, Jesus reassures us that these wars and rumors of wars have to happen, but that they do not indicate, by their occurrence, alone, that the end of the age is at hand. That is to say, Jesus wanted us to know that we have to look for the remaining five *signs* which will occur after these wars and rumors of wars, to know that these confirm the Beginning of Sorrows.

Of course, the wars and rumors of wars will continue to happen throughout the occurrence of the following five world events, and all seven occurring at the same time is the key for us being able to identify the Beginning of Sorrows and the *approximate* time of Jesus's preludial rapture of the Christian church from the earth; that is to say, we know that the rapture is going to happen after the seven global signs but before the start of the tribulation—or *wrath*—period.

How can we know and confirm these truths? By biblical scriptures, we are informed of them and can take comfort in the same. In 1 Thessalonians 5:9, we are told that, "God did not appoint us for wrath." And, in Romans 8:1, our security is underpinned with the promise that, "There is, therefore, no condemnation to those who are in Christ Jesus." In both these, we can know that the tribulation period was not established for us, nor should we be fearful that we must endure it since we are redeemed by our God.

So let us look at the first significant aspect of Matthew 24:6 a bit closer. Why did Jesus say that we would only *hear* of wars and rumors of wars, and not see them, as we would the other global events occurring? And, why did He tell us not to be troubled when we did hear of them? In my opinion, these statements are critical in identifying not only the prophesied *generation* (which I have already advanced as Generation X) but also the period in time and a country where the vast majority of that Christian generation is dwelling—and observing from—during the prophetic *season*.

Getting right to the point, I believe that Generation X is the generation of Christian believers that Jesus foretold would be the witnesses to the seven global events which mark the Beginning of Sorrows (and thus, we have been since the 1990s with the worldwide proliferation of technologies), and that, America is the home base for Christian observers of those Beginning of Sorrows—*signs*.

Moreover, I believe that Jesus specifically identified America in Matthew 24:6, when He told us that "you will hear" of the wars and rumors of wars but then told us not to be "troubled" by that news when we do. In essence, Jesus was telling us that these wars which

He prophesied of will take place in their appointed times, but that they would not be taking place on the soil of our nation, wherefrom, the vast majority of the world's evangelical Christians now hail. Jesus knew that the vast number of modern-day disciples would be right here in the United States during the Beginning of Sorrows, that God would be blessing us as a Nation, and that our military capabilities would be such that no foreign country would dare attack us—by means of an all-out assault—on our own soil, during this point of prophetic events unfolding. That is why He wanted us to know—in advance—that we should not be troubled when we started hearing of these wars and rumors of wars because they would not be taking place on American soil. If they were going to occur here in America, I believe that Jesus would not have told us that we—as the observing generation—would only "hear" of them, but rather He would have warned us that we would be "seeing" them in this season, just the way that many other countries are now; at this point in time, I believe that Jesus wanted to provide us (as the vigilant Christian observers) with a measure of comfort in the time that identifies the Beginning of Sorrows, by letting us know that these wars would not present a physical threat to our safety and security.

So why America one may ask? Because contrary to all that is being taught in our nation's schools and colleges and universities across this great country, and reinforced by those in governmental positions of power who themselves deny God, and lead others to do the same, God is alive, and this nation was founded on Christian beliefs and moralities which have served to define who we are as a people among the other nations of the world. Indeed, our founding forefathers and foremothers, who abandoned their own heritages and homelands to set course for a land which they did not know, did so with the hope of creating for themselves and their posterity a new home, one that was dedicated to God, where they could be free to acknowledge and worship Him and as a result be blessed by Him.

I conclude it to be no coincidence then that with a population of over 331 million people, currently, America is the motherland to more than 225 million self-identifying Christian believers, about 68 percent of the overall population. There is no other country on the face of the earth that can boast such a diversified Christian population within its borders as America has. Moreover, it is because of our beginnings that our national hope is that "God Bless[es] America" and why Congress declared our national *motto* to be "In God We Trust" in 1956.

There can be no quarrel against the allegation that many in our nation's distant past, and more in these end times, it seems, have fought tirelessly to detach God's name from the social fabric of our national identity, and we will continue to see these kinds of anti-God assaults increasing as we draw closer to the end of the age and our Lord's second coming to the earth. However, as long as there remains a Christian remnant in this great country, I believe that God's name and Spirit will not depart from it. In short, I believe that this country was chosen for this hour, by God, because it is a nation that, from its roots, cries out for Him to use and bless it.

Turning our attention back to the prophecy of "wars and rumors of wars," when many of us think of "war" nowadays, we envision one country attacking another with tanks and warships and aircraft of all sorts, as opposed to different groups or countries facing off on a battlefield of times past and armed with clubs and swords or rifles. It may come as a surprise to many of us to learn that in many third-world countries, these seemingly primitive means of war are still used.

For our understanding of Jesus's prophecy, it is prudent for us to first learn what the true definition of war is. Looking to the *Concise Oxford English Dictionary: 11ᵗʰ Ed. Revised © Oxford University Press 2008*, we discover that *war* is defined as "a state of armed conflict between different countries or different groups within a country." Given this definition of what constitutes war, we can understand that it encompasses both armed civil conflicts, at one end of the continuum, with full-scale international conflicts at the other, and everything in between.

Armed with the definition for *war*, we can now redirect our attention to the question of whether or not we have heard, and are now hearing, of the "wars and rumors of wars," which Jesus told us that we would be when those Beginning of Sorrows—events are occurring. The timeline that we must focus on is between the 1990s and present if we intend to carry the analytical proposition that Generation X is *the generation* who started to witness the prophecy unfold. So have wars, and the rumors of possible wars, taken place since the 1990s to the present? The short answer to that question is yes, so let us take a look at a few of them that have occurred since 1990 and which may stand out in our memories.

Persian Gulf War—1990

On August 2, 1990, Iraqi Dictator Saddam Hussein invaded the country of Kuwait and annexed it. The United Nations Security Council ordered Iraqi forces to leave Kuwait by January 15, 1991. When Saddam Hussein refused to withdraw from Kuwait, a US-led multinational force, known as Operation Desert Storm, unleashed a heavy bombardment of munitions on military targets in Kuwait and Iraq. With the execution of a coordinated air-land offensive, dubbed Operation Desert Sabre, which began on February 24, 1991, the US and her allies retook Kuwait City on February 26, 1991, and a permanent cease-fire was signed on April 6, 1991. The US military forces suffered approximately 150 *battle deaths* during Operation Desert Storm. As a result of limited technologies for publicizing the war to civilian populations in 1990 through 1991, that being radio and television only, for those who could afford them, the world community did not enjoy a play-by-play briefing of developments related to the 1990 Persian Gulf War on a wide scale.

War on terror—2001

In October 2000, the USS *Cole* (a US warship) was attacked by means of a suicide bombing—leaving seventeen service personnel dead—in Aden, Yemen. US Intelligence sources determined that the attack was tied to Al-Qaeda (a terrorist network that had made its base in Afghanistan) and that the Taliban (the fundamentalist Muslim movement that ruled much of Afghanistan) was harboring them. As *part* of America's response to the terrorist attack on the warship, a US-led military coalition ousted the Taliban regime from its position of power in Afghanistan, and a "transitional government" was installed in December 2001. In August 2003, NATO was handed control over multinational forces. Recently, under President Joe Biden, US Combat Troops were withdrawn from Afghanistan, which stranded many Americans and resulted in needless loss of life. Because of the proliferation of advanced technologies by 2000, much of the military activity which took place in Afghanistan was publicized for humanity at large to see and hear, both good and bad.

War in Iraq—2003

On September 11, 2001, Middle Eastern hijackers crashed two jetliners into the twin towers called the World Trade Center in New York City, another into the US Pentagon outside Washington, DC, with a fourth crashing in a field in Pennsylvania. The four acts of terrorism killed nearly three thousand people and were eventually linked to Osama bin Laden, the founder and leader of the Al-Qaeda terrorist network. The actions of Osama bin Laden worked to prime the hearts and minds of most Americans for war, and in 2002, after President George W. Bush accused the country of Iraq of developing weapons of mass destruction (WMDs), the US and her trusted ally, the United Kingdom, invaded Iraq in March 2003, to forcibly remove the Ba'athist regime in power and set up a democratic government, as an extension of the US's war-on-terrorism campaign. It may come as a surprise to many to learn that the war on terrorism is a US-led military campaign that has been ongoing for nearly twenty-two years, since 2001. That is to say, US military forces are still actively hunting down and eliminating known terrorist cells all across the face of the planet on a consistent basis. The war on terrorism has no foreseeable *cease-fire* date.

Counting those listed above, the world has seen 174 documented *wars* since 1990 to the present, with a staggering 45 of them still ongoing at the time that this page of the book was being inscribed. America has had a part to one extent or another—in 59 of those 174 wars. Below, we can review a list of ongoing wars since 1990:

Start date   Name of war/ conflict

- 1990   DBKP/C insurgency in Turkey
- 1991   Somali Civil War
- 1993   Ethnic conflict in Nagaland
- 1994   Armenian-Azerbaijani border conflict (part of the Nagorno-Karabakh conflict)
- 1994   Chiapas conflict
- 1996   ADF insurgency
- 1998   Al-Qaeda insurgency in Yemen
- 2001   War on terrorism
- 2002   Operation Enduring Freedom—Horn of Africa
- 2002   Taliban insurgency (Part of the War in Afghanistan)
- 2003   War in Darfur
- 2004   Conflict in the Niger Delta
- 2004   Kivu conflict
- 2004   Sistan and Baluchestan insurgency (part of the Balochistan conflict)
- 2005   Paraguayan People's Army insurgency
- 2006   Fatah-Hamas conflict
- 2006   Mexican Drug War
- 2007   Operation Enduring Freedom—Trans Sahara
- 2009   Sudanese Nomadic conflicts
- 2009   Boko Haram insurgency
- 2009   South Yemen insurgency
- 2009   Somali Civil War
- 2011   Sinai insurgency
- 2011   Syrian Civil War

- 2011   Sudanese conflict in South Kordofan and Blue Nile
- 2011   Ethnic violence in South Sudan
- 2012   Northern Mali conflict
- 2012   Central African Republic conflict
- 2014   Libyan Civil War
- 2014   War in Donbass
- 2014   International military intervention against ISIL
- 2015   Yemeni Civil War
- 2015   ISIL insurgency in Tunisia
- 2015   Kurdish-Turkish conflict
- 2016   2016 Niger Delta conflict
- 2016   Northern Rakhine State clashes (part of the Rohingya insurgency in Western Myanmar and the internal conflict in Myanmar)
- 2016   Kamwina Nsapu rebellion
- 2017   2017–2020 Qatif unrest (part of the Qatif conflict)
- 2017   Anglophone Crisis
- 2017   Islamist insurgency in Mozambique
- 2017   Iraqi insurgency (2017 to present)
- 2018   War in Catatumbo
- 2019   2019–2020 Persian Gulf Crisis
- 2020   2020 China-India armed skirmishes
- 2022   Russian-Ukrainian War (2022 to present)

This *partial list* of wars was taken from a complete list provided on Wikipedia®. A Google © search of "List of Wars" will provide the viewer with additional websites that publish and maintain a list of conflicts which have occurred and that are continuing to take place at this time, but I have chosen to rely on Wikipedia® for all the reasons, which were previously explained in the second chapter of this book. With that said, I support all additional research into the matter for any reader who is motivated to do so, especially if the reason for it is because of lingering questions over whether or not the sign—

one of seven global events that are prophesied by Jesus to reveal the Beginning of Sorrows—is now fulfilled by current wars.

There can be no serious argument made against the demonstrated proposition that there have been "wars and rumors of wars" taking place since the beginning of 1990 when Generation X would have reached young adulthood and that at least forty-five of those wars are ongoing at this time. Moreso, there can be no fact-based argument made against the position that these wars are taking place on a global scale and at the same time as the first prophetic sign that we covered in the last chapter. In light of the facts, it is with no difficulty that we can conclude that the *second sign* that foretells of "wars and rumors of wars" is occurring now, and we are encouraged to move forward with analyzing the *third sign*.

WARS AND RUMORS OF WARS ☑

CHAPTER 4

Global Rise in Racial Tensions and Conflicts

For nation shall rise against nation.

—Matthew 24:7

IN THIS PORTION of the prophecy, we are told of conflicts that begin taking place between nation(s)—*on a global scale*—at the Beginning of Sorrows. These conflicts are the third sign, which Jesus told us to watch for so that we would know the season that we were in. Our modern American use of the word *nation* is for what is defined as a *country* these days, but a country is not what Jesus was speaking about when He used the word *nation* in this verse. The use of the word *nation* here in this scripture actually refers to a race of people.

For clarification purposes, we reference the *Concise Oxford English Dictionary: 11ᵗʰ Edition Revised © Oxford University Press 2008*, which defines *nation* as "a large body of people united by *common descent, culture,* or [a] language, inhabiting a particular state or territory." Moreover, we can be sure that Jesus was referring to conflicts between the races, instead of actual countries, by the verse that comes next, where Jesus goes on to explain that: "And Kingdom [shall rise] against kingdom" (Matthew 24:7). Jesus's use of the word *kingdom* actually refers to modern-day countries, so His prior use of the word *nation* would not. I understand that all this can get to be a bit confusing, so for the purposes of this chapter, all that we need to remember is that the word *nation* = race. With this established, Jesus's statement would read like this: "For race shall rise against race…" So in plain English, the prophecy spoken by Jesus foretells that, at the time of the Beginning of Sorrows, in addition to the previously discussed signs of Jesus's impostors and wars occurring on a global scale, at the same time, we will see a rise in racial tensions and conflicts taking place.

For most now reading this book, one does not have to look too hard to confirm that we are seeing this portion of the prophecy being fulfilled in nearly every country on the face of the earth, including right here on the streets of America. In 2020, we were witnesses to a rise in racial tensions and conflicts here in the United States, the likes of which have not been seen since the 1960s and 1970s, but in unprecedented numbers. These tensions and conflicts manifested in the forms of race-filled protests, civil disobedience, clashes, assaults, riots, thefts, and mobs' destruction of private and public properties, in nearly every major city across America. Soon after they had begun happening, here, countries around the world started reporting similar kinds of occurrences taking place among their citizenry. Most, if not all, of these racially motivated occurrences, can be tied to one (now globally recognized) driving force called the Black Lives Matter (BLM) movement.

On July 13, 2013, Alicia Garza, Patrisse Cullors, and Opal Tometi began an "anti-racist advocacy and protest" movement that is named Black Lives Matter (BLM), with their publication of the hashtag #BlackLivesMatter, after the acquittal of a White man, George Zimmerman, in the shooting death of an African American teen, Trayvon Martin, in February 2012. The Black Lives Matter (BLM) movement gained national attention in 2014, following its street demonstrations held in response to the deaths of two more African American men: Michael Brown and Eric Garner.

Since its inception, the Black Lives Matter (BLM) movement has called for and supported protests and demonstrations in response to what is believed to be the unjustified killings and deaths of at least thirty-six African American men and women and children, by White men and police officers, namely, Trayvon Martin (2012),

Michael Brown (2014), Eric Garner (2014), Dontre Hamilton (2014), Ezell Ford (2014), Tamir Rice (2014), Akai Gurley (2014), Laquan McDonald (2014), Antonio Martin (2014), Jerame Reid (2014), John Crawford III (2014), Renisha McBride (2014), Charley Leundeu Keunang (2015), Anthony Hill (2015), Tony Robinson (2015), Meagan Hockaday (2015), Eric Harris (2015), Walter Scott (2015), Freddie Gray (2015), William Chapman (2015), Jonathan Sanders (2015), Sandra Bland (2015), Samuel DuBose (2015), Jeremy McDole (2015), Corey Jones (2015), Jamar Clark (2015), Aiyana Jones (2015), Rekia Boyd (2015), Timothy Russell (2015), Malissa Williams (2015), Jonathan Ferrell (2015), Alton Sterling (2016), Philando Castile (2016), Stephon Clark (2018), Breonna Taylor (2020), and George Floyd (2020).

Out of these thirty-six men and women and children mentioned above, several of their stories made national headlines as a direct result of the protests and demonstrations organized by the Black Lives Matter (BLM) movement. Many of us still recall the heartbreaking stories of Eric Garner, Michael Brown, Tamir Rice, Walter Scott, Alton Sterling, Philando Castile, Stephon Clark, Breonna Taylor, and George Floyd, whose lives were cut short as a result of racism in some cases and overreaction in others. It was these victims' stories that drew international attention and worked to elevate racial tensions and conflicts across the United States and around the world.

Eric Garner died on July 17, 2014, after being wrestled to the ground by a New York police officer on suspicion of illegally selling cigarettes. The police officer had placed Mr. Garner in a choke hold and refused to loosen the pressure despite the fact that Mr. Garner cried out eleven times, "I can't breathe." A fellow citizen filmed the unjustified police killing.

Michael Brown was killed by a police officer in Ferguson, Missouri, on August 9, 2014, after the police officer responded to a call that Mr. Brown had stolen a box of cigars from a local convenience store. The police officer shot Mr. Brown six times during the encounter.

Tamir Rice, who was only twelve years old at the time of his death, on November 22, 2014, was shot dead by a police officer after the police officer received a call that a *juvenile* was pointing a gun that was *probably fake* at passersby, in the city of Cleveland, Ohio.

Walter Scott, who died on April 4, 2015, was shot in the back five times by a police officer after being pulled over for having a defective light on his car in North Charleston, South Carolina. Mr. Scott was trying to run away from the police officer after a brief scuffle between the two.

Alton Sterling was killed by Baton Rouge, Louisiana, police on July 5, 2016, after police responded to a call involving a disturbance outside of a small shop.

Philando Castile was killed by police on July 6, 2016, when he and his girlfriend were pulled over in St. Paul, Minnesota, during a *routine check*. Mr. Castile was shot to death when he reached for his driver's license, according to his girlfriend.

Stephon Clark died on March 18, 2018, after police officers in Sacramento, California, shot him at least seven times while they were reportedly investigating a break-in.

Breonna Taylor, a twenty-six-year-old emergency medical technician (EMT), was shot by police officers eight times, when officers raided her apartment in Louisville, Kentucky, on March 13, 2020. Police claimed that they were executing a search warrant for drugs, but no drugs were discovered in Ms. Taylor's residence.

George Floyd was killed on May 25, 2020, after being arrested in Minneapolis, Minnesota, as a result of being held down by four police officers, one of which had his knee on Mr. Floyd's neck, preventing him from breathing. Mr. Floyd cried out in agonizing distress for his mother, who had been deceased for three years prior to his killing. Bystanders recorded the entire encounter by cell phone video.

Just today, as this page of the book is being written, local and national news organizations are reporting on another police shooting of an unarmed Black man out in Columbus, Ohio, by a White police officer. Andre Hill, the forty-five-year-old victim, was reportedly shot dead as he was exiting the garage of his family's home while holding a cell phone in his left hand, with the lit screen deliberately facing forward so that it could not be easily mistaken for being anything other than what it was when the officer opened fire. The White police officer did not activate his *body cam* to capture the encounter until *after* Mr. Hill had been gunned down. A feature on the body cam caused sixty seconds of the time prior to its manual activation to be recorded, revealing that Mr. Hill did not do anything to justify or otherwise provoke the police officer's action of shooting him.

An update on this story shared a video interview of Mr. Hill's daughter and spouse expressing their dismay and grief over the loss of this beloved father and husband. The daughter is seen in the news interview wearing a "Black Lives Matter (BLM)" beanie and supplicating for justice in her father's killing. There can be little doubt that this kind of racial-biased police killing will replay in the near future, as it has done time and again, and it begs the question of how many more innocent lives will be stolen in this way, and how much more will the Black community take before they take a widespread violent stand, and demand "an eye for an eye" and a "tooth for a tooth"? We must ask ourselves as White and Brown Americans, how much we would take if it were our fathers, mothers, sons, and daughters being gunned down and mistreated?

The racial tension between Whites and Blacks around the world has never been more pronounced and grave, and it shows no promise of abating. A racial line has been drawn in the proverbial sand, and both sides seem to be daring their *perceived* enemy to cross it. International and national news organizations, democratically ran television networks, and our world leaders fan the flames of this rising racial unrest, for the purpose of earning high ratings and accomplishing their self-serving political agendas, while acts of lawlessness and chaos lay waste to the communities of many major cities around the globe.

A widely spreading and accepted phenomenon that is difficult for many White Americans to understand is that a growing number of minorities in America look at—and consider—all police officers as being *White*, despite their true individual ethnicity, and so any officer-involved killing of an African American is looked at by these Americans of color as being perpetuated by a racist White person or persons. Of course, then, this phenomenon is working to create feelings of racial injustice in those who may not otherwise be inclined to feel that way and a desire for them to take action.

Ironically, however, if a White or Black or Brown police officer shoots and kills a White American, there is no such viewpoint taken in that incident; the police officer that shoots the White victim is neither viewed as being Black or Brown or any other race than what they actually are nor predetermined to have been racially motivated in so doing. For example, in 2019, there were 1,001 American civilians killed by authorities in the United States. Of those killed, approximately half are known to have been White men and women, and about one-third were Black. In every case involving a White victim, not one public accusation was made alleging that the police officer was racially motivated when he or she caused the death of the White decedent, regardless of the officer's race.

This manufactured viewpoint is dangerous because it divides Americans—and the global communities—and creates an "us versus them" state of mind in those who embrace it. There is no doubt that America has racist White police officers serving in departments across this country and that there are some of them that unjustly gun down and otherwise mistreat those in Black communities. With that said, we also have racist Black and Brown officers that gun down and mistreat White people under the color of law. Point is, it is a bad-cop issue, not a bad-race issue. Reprehensibly, the Black Lives Matter (BLM) organizers and spokespeople are using this dangerous and false rhetoric (that all police officers are White racists that want to gun down and mistreat African Americans) to gather support for their mission. Therefore, we should all come together as one in rejecting this false outlook since common sense and reality alone defeats it.

The overall Black Lives Matter (BLM) movement is understood to be a decentralized international network of activists that has no formal hierarchy, operating around the world in countries such as Canada, Australia, New Zealand, Germany, Denmark, Japan, and the United Kingdom, as well as the United States. It is thought to have been established to respond to sustained and increasingly visible violence against Black communities in the United States and abroad. Notwithstanding many of its supporters and participants being men and women and children of other races, the main focus of the movement has been—and most assuredly will remain—centered on the injustices perpetuated by *perceived* White *racist* actors and the police. In the course of holding protests and demonstrations calling out and condemning police killings and mistreatment of Blacks, supporters hold up signs with political slogans which include the following: "Black Lives Matter," "White Silence Is Violence," "No Justice, No Peace," "Defund the Police," "I Can't Breathe," and "Not One More," just to name a few.

In all sincerity, I submit that the Black Lives Matter (BLM) movement is more than a network of activists trying to bring our attention to injustices against Black communities throughout the world. Realistically—and in fact—the movement is a well-funded "Black Power" *army* that is calling its soldiers to *fall in* and prepare for battle for if, and when, diplomacy is deemed to have failed, and thus, abandoned, and the time calls for it, just as any race of people would do if they believed that they were being unjustly and systematically slaughtered and abused by a different governing race. In truth, the movement is activating their Black communities' primal survival instincts, by intentionally, and consistently, waving their enemy's alleged atrocities against the Black race in their faces, a military technique used throughout history to enrage and prepare soldiers for war. Directly after the unjustified killing of George Floyd, during the protests and demonstrations that followed, we witnessed a *flicker* of reprisal for the centuries of wrongs inflicted upon the Black communities of the world, but make no mistake about it; there are *wildfires* igniting in the moral drought, and the Black Lives Matter (BLM) movement is the strong winds that drive them.

In America, there is a real and growing effort by the Black Lives Matter (BLM) movement and its supporters to reach out for, and seize, political power at the highest levels of our state and federal governments. The proponents of this effort see it as a means of obtaining a form of reparations for a plethora of wrongs inflicted upon Black America, by White America, in a review of our nation's history—a "struggle between good and evil" as it were. The strength and focus of this ongoing effort were exemplified in the outcome of the 2020 elections, where it was realized that we, as a country, are divided into two major groups with completely different visions for the future of America. Many White members of our current state and federal governments have chosen to align themselves with the movement in an effort to maintain their voter support and, thereby, cling firmly to their positions of power, while others tirelessly fight in resistance to the changing times threatened. The "White supremacists" and "Black Power" extremist organizations in America are energized at levels, which have not been seen in fifty years, and take every opportunity to add fuel to these ever-growing social wildfires.

There are few, if any, that would reject the conclusion that we have been witnessing a drastic global rise in racial tensions and conflicts. The *third sign* of Jesus's prophecy from Matthew 24:7 is now occurring, and the scriptures warn us that these kinds of clashes will only spread and become even more violent in the months and years to come, as we approach the tribulation period and end of time.

In America, the political aspirations of the Black Lives Matter (BLM) movement, to seize power and establish a more Black culture-friendly government, will work to fuel the rage of White supremacists groups whose members are willing to take whatever steps that they deem are necessary to prevent that takeover, all the way up to, and including, terrorist attacks and civil war. We as believers would do well to monitor these racial schisms and conflicts (as we should also do with the other six prophetic *signs*) but to stay mindful of the fact that the world government which they long to control will give way to Jesus's government that He is coming soon to set up, and so we have no true interest in supporting either side. This is important for our mandate to maintain unity within the church, while the world around us encourages dissent and falls.

NATION AGAINST NATION ☑

CHAPTER 5

Civil Unrest and Insurrection

And kingdom against kingdom.

—Matthew 24:7

THE SECOND HALF of verse seven speaks of "kingdom(s)" rising up against one another as being one of the seven *signs* that occur at the Beginning of Sorrows. In times past, most have understood this portion of the prophecy to mean that there will be a rise in tensions and conflicts taking place between *countries* at the start of the prophetic *season*, but that interpretation of this second half of verse seven is proved inaccurate based on one plain fact found in the prophecy itself, which is Jesus had already covered a rise in tensions and conflicts between countries earlier in the chapter, in verse 6, "Wars and rumors of wars" (Matthew 24:6). Therefore, it is illogical to assume that Jesus would needlessly, and superfluously, state a separate warning about the same events in the same chapter. Jesus's warning here, in the second half of verse seven, does not refer to countries rising up against other countries but rather warns of the populations of the countries around the world rising up against their governments (i.e., civil unrest and insurrections [violent uprisings against authorities]).

In light of the foregoing interpretation, we are obligated to investigate and discover evidence that establishes that there are global occurrences of civil unrest and insurrections taking place at this time if we are to decisively conclude that we are now witnessing the *fourth sign* illuminating the Beginning of Sorrows.

The citizens of the world as we know it feels more lost confused, hopeless, helpless, and angry than they ever have felt in remembrance of times past, right now. Many have no idea what is going on with the occurrence of catastrophe after the catastrophe that is plaguing the nations of the earth, from wars and famines and newly emerging diseases, and most have an expectation that things are only going to get worse from this point moving forward, both in the short-term and long-term.

An element compounding this unprecedented state of hopelessness and global uncertainty is the fact that many of us no longer trust our elected government officials to help the situation and to do the jobs that they have been placed in their respective offices to do, and those who are currently at the controls of these world governments seem to be just as lost and grimly apprehensive about the future as the people whom they are governing. It reminds me of the Bible verse referring to "the blind leading the blind." As a result of this lack of strong and effective leadership, over the past few years, recent world history records and current national and global news broadcasts reports are replete with documented instances of widespread civil unrest sweeping across the face of our planet, manifesting in the form of civil protest and violence against those established governmental powers that be. Indeed, we can see and feel a global appetite for civil rebellion growing.

These newly dubbed *social movements* and modern-day societal revolutionary efforts can be understood to range on a continuum from moderate to mass-sized protests intended to induce policy change on one end and up to large-scale highly sophisticated schemes to topple heads of state and replace them with de facto leaders at the extreme end. Some have speculated that the cause of most of the global uncertainty and discontent has a direct connection to the emergence and global spread of COVID-19 and its seemingly endless *variants* plaguing humanity; that is, many believe that COVID-19 is the cause of all our current troubles.

The motivation for these sizable civil modern-day protests, which we have seen on television and/or live-streaming Internet broadcasts, is to force our world leaders to take note of and rectify significant social issues and injustices that are seemingly commonplace in this day and age in most societies around the world. There is no need here to provide evidence or examples of these large-scale anti-government protests, since we all have seen and/or heard of them taking place. Ergo, I will not waste time and resources providing unnecessary information; instead, I will focus on the extreme end of the social movement continuum, since that information is not as widely reported on, or known by, most in society.

The term *coup d'état* or *coup* for short (which is defined as "a sudden violent seizure of power from government") has found its way into some of the aforementioned modern-day history records and news reporting. The term is assigned to efforts by organized actors to take over government seats of power by force. This is the most extreme way for the people of a state or nation (or "Kingdom"), those who govern over them. Moreover, the act of attempting to do so is defined as *high treason*, punishable by death.

With this definition of *coup* in mind, we can now turn to the Internet for ease in locating information which might assist us in determining whether or not there is evidence in our present time of this extreme form of "Kingdom ris[ing] against kingdom"; that is, citizens rising up against their governments to seize power from the same. By Googling® the phrase, "List of Coups and Coup Attempts by Country," we discover that Wikipedia® provides us with a chronological list of countries, which have experienced these types of extreme and violent events in recent times. A review reveals a total of 119 coups and coup attempts from 1990 to the present day. Below, I have duplicated some of the relevant information which can be found on this Wikipedia® website:

Country	Date and Coup or Coup Attempt
Afghanistan	March 6, 1990: Shahnawaz Tanai attempts and fails to overthrow Mohammad Najibullah
	August 15, 2021: Withdrawal of US forces allows the 2021 Taliban offensive to overthrow the government of Ashraf Ghani and reinstate the Islamic Emirate of Afghanistan

Albania	September 14, 1998: The funeral of MP Azem Hajdari turns violent as the office of the Albanian Prime Minister Fatos Nano is attacked/obliging the latter to hastily flee and step down shortly after
Algeria	January 11, 1992: Khaled Nezzar overthrows Chadli Bendjedid
Armenia	February 25, 2021: the Armenian military calls for Prime Minister Nikol Pashinyan to resign. Pashinyan accuses the military of attempting a coup d'état
Azerbaijan	June 9, 1993: Heydar Aliyev overthrows Abulfaz Elchibey in a political crisis during the first Nagorno-Karabakh War March 13, 1995: Colonel Rovshan Javadov and his unit of OPON troops fail to seize power from President Heydar Aliyev and reinstate his predecessor Abulfaz Elchibey after Turkish President Suleyman Demirel warned Aliyev
Bangladesh	May 7, 1995: Abu Saleh Mohammad Nasim attempts and fails to overthrow Abdur Rahman Biswas January 11, 2007: General Moeen U Ahmed pressures President Iajuddin Ahmed into declaring a state of emergency, postponing elections/ and appointing a new Chief Advisor to head the caretaker government December 2011: Rebel army officers attempt and fail to overthrow Sheikh Hasina
Benin	March 4, 2013: Failed coup attempt by Colonel Pamphile Zomahoun against President Thomas Boni Yayi

Bolivia	2019 Bolivian political crisis: Evo Morales was told to step down by the military and police following political unrest in response to a report by the Organization of American States which alleged that there were irregularities in the 2019 Bolivian general election. Morales resigned with his entire cabinet and legislative leaders.
Bophuthatswana	March 11, 1994: Lucas Mangope is overthrown by mutinying Bophuthatswana Defence Force forces supported by the South African Defence Force. Bophuthatswana, a Bantustan established during apartheid, is reincorporated into South Africa
Burkina Faso	October 30, 2014: Lt. Colonel Yacouba Isaac Zida overthrows current President Blaise Compaoré and briefly serves as head of state before selecting Michel Kafando as the new president. Days later, Kafando appointed Zida as acting Prime Minister
	September 17, 2015: The presidential guard headed by Gilbert Diendéré overthrows Interim President Michel Kafando, one month before elections are due in the nation. However, the coup collapses one week later and Kafando is reinstalled
Burundi	July 25, 1995: Pierre Buyoya overthrows Sylvestre Ntibantunganya
	May 13–15, 2015: Failed coup d'etat led by General Godefroid Niyombare against President Pierre Nkurunziza
Cambodia	July 5, 1997: Hun Sen overthrows Norodom Ranariddh

Central African Republic	1996: Soldiers attempt to overthrow Patassé May 27–28, 2001: Failed attempt against Ange-Felix Patassé October 8–25, 2001: Francois Bozizé attempts to overthrow Patassé March 15, 2003: Francois Bozizé overthrows Francois Bozize December 2020–January 2021: Failed coup attempt by rebel groups led by Francois Bozizé against Faustin-Archange Touadéra
Chad	December 1, 1990: Idriss Déby overthrows Hisséne Habré May 16, 2004: Failed coup against President Idriss Déby March 14, 2006: Failed coup against President Idriss Déby May 1, 2013: Failed coup against Idriss Déby
Ciskei	March 4, 1990: Oupa Gqozo and the Ciskei Defense Force overthrow Lennox Sebe
Comoros	September 28, 1995: Bob Denard overthrows Said Mohamed Djohar for seven days (see Operation Azalee) April 30, 1999: Azali Assoumani overthrows Tadjidine Ben Said Massounde April 20, 2013: A failed coup against President Ikililou Dhoinine
Congo, Democratic Republic of the	May 16, 1997: Laurent-Desire Kabila overthrows Mobutu Sese Seko, leading to the first Congo War
Congo, Republic of the	October 25, 1997: Denis Sassou Nguesso overthrows Pascal Lissouba
Ecuador	2000: Coup by Lucio Gutierrez

Egypt	2011: Hosni Mubarak is overthrown 2013: Mohamed Morsi overthrown by General Abdel Fattah El Sisi
El Salvador	May 1, 2021: Self-coup by the Legislative Assembly
Equatorial Guinea	March 7, 2004: A coup attempt is stopped before the plotters can arrive in the country
Ethiopia	June 22, 2019: Failed coup against the regional government in Amhara Region; resulted in the death of several prominent Ethiopian civil and military officials
Fiji	May 19, 2000: George Speight overthrows Mahendra Chaudhry December 5, 2006: Frank Bainimarama overthrows Laisenia Qarase
Gabon	January 7, 2019: Gabonese soldiers seize the national radio in an attempted coup against Ali Bongo Ondimba
Gambia	July 22, 1994: Yahya Jammeh overthrows Dawda Jawara December 30, 2014: A failed coup against Yahya Jammeh led by the former head of the presidential guards Lamin Sanneh
Guinea	December 24, 2008: Moussa Dadis Camara overthrows Aboubacar Somparé September 5, 2021: Mamady Doumbouya overthrows Alpha Condé
Guinea-Bissau	May 7, 1999: Ansumane Mané overthrows João Bernardo Vieria September 14, 2003: Verissimo Correia Seabra overthrows Kumba Ialá April 12, 2012: Army overthrows the government

Haiti	September 30, 1991: Raoul Cédras overthrows Jean-Bertrand Aristide
	February 5–29, 2004: Ousted President Jean-Bertrand Aristide during his second term
Honduras	2009: Coup of leadership.
Indonesia	May 1998: Riots in Indonesia
Ivory Coast	December 24, 1999: Robert Guei overthrows Henri Konan Bédié
Jordan	2021: Failed coup attempt by Prince Hamzah bin Hussein to overthrow his half-brother/ King Abdullah II
Loas	2007: Laotian coup failed coup by General Vang Pao
Lesotho	November 12, 1990: Justin Metsing Lekhanya overthrows King Moshoeshoe II of Lesotho
	May 2, 1991: Elias Phisoana Ramaema overthrows Justin Metsing Lekhanya
	August 30, 2014: A failed coup attempt
Liberia	September 9, 1990: Prince Johnson overthrows President Samuel K. Doe
Libya	April 17, 2013: An attempt Libyan coup against Prime Minister Ali Zeidan by Muammar Gaddafi loyalists
	October 10, 2013: A second attempt Libyan coup led by Abdel-Moneim al-Hour against Prime Minister Ali Zeidan
	April and October 2014: A failed coups against Prime Minister Ali Zeidan in first coup and Prime Minister Abdullah al-Thani in second coup by Maj. Gen. Khalifa Haftar
	October 2016: A failed coup against Prime Minister Fayez al-Sarraj by ex-Prime Minister Khalifa al-Ghawil

Madagascar	March 17, 2009: Rajoelina overthrows Marc Ravalomanana (see 2009 Malagasy political crisis)
Mali	March 26, 1991: Amadou Toumani Touré overthrows Moussa Traoré March 22, 2012: Military overthrows Amadou Toumani Touré August 18, 2020: Military overthrows Ibrahim Boubacar Keita 2021: Malian coup d'état; military overthrows Bah N'daw
Mauritania	August 3, 2005: Ely Ould Mohamed Vall overthrows Maaouya Ould Sid'Ahmed Taya August 6, 2008: Mohamed Ould Abdel Aziz overthrows Sidi Ould Cheikh Abdallah
Montenegro	October 2016: Attempted coup by opposition and Russian agents against the government of Milo Đukanović on the day of parliamentary election
Myanmar (Burma)	February 1, 2021: Min Aung Hlaing attempts to overthrow Aung San Suu Kyi
Nepal	February 2005: King Gyanendra dismissed the parliament of Nepal and declared a state of emergency
Niger	January 27, 1996: Ibrahim Baré Mainassara overthrows Mahamane Ousmane April 9, 1999: Daouda Malam Wanké overthrows Ibrahim Baré Mainassara
Nigeria	April 22, 1990: Gideon Orkar failed to topple President Ibrahim Babangida November 17, 1993: Sani Abacha overthrows Ernest Shonekan

Pakistan	1995: A group of Pakistani Armed Forces officers led by Zahirul Islam Abbasi plot to overthrow the Pakistan People's Party government of Benazir Bhutto
	October 12, 1999: General Pervez Musharraf overthrows the PML-N government Prime Minister Nawaz Sharif and suspends the writ of the Constitution because of Sharif's intent to relieve him as Chairman of the Joint Chiefs of Staff
Peru	1992: Under Alberto Fujimori (self-coup)
Philippines	March 4, 1990: Hotel Delfino siege, government troops under Brigadier General Oscar Florendo fought against rebel forces led by suspended Cagayan Governor Rodolfo "Agi" Aguinaldo, crushed by the Philippine government
	October 4–6, 1990: Failed mutiny as the Mindanao crisis, mutinying soldiers staged a dawn raid on an army base in Mindanao, defeated by the government
	January 17–20, 2001: Successful Second EDSA Revolution: a four-day political protest was held in EDSA, that peacefully overthrow the government of President Joseph Estrada
	April 25–May 1, 2001: Failed EDSA III; a seven-day political protest was held also in EDSA, in a failed attempt to bring back Joseph Estrada to power
	July 27, 2003: Failed Oakwood mutiny, failed coup attempt with mutinous soldiers surrendering after taking over the Oakwood condominiums in the Makati Central Business District

February 24, 2006: State of emergency to forestall alleged coup against the government

November 29, 2007: Failed Manila Peninsula siege, mutinous soldiers occupied the Peninsula Manila Hotel, later surrendered to the government

(Alleged plot that has not been attempted yet, below)

2018–present: Allegations of an ouster plot against President Rodrigo Duterte were first publicized by the military, which mainly implicated the opposition figures and the critics of the Duterte administration of involvement in the plot

Russia

August 19–21, 1991: A group of Soviet Communist Party hardliners form the State Committee of the State of Emergency and attempt to overthrow President Mikhail Gorbachev to reverse his reforms: the coup is suppressed by RSFSR President Boris Yeltsin, weakening the Communist Party's authority and accelerating the dissolution of the Soviet Union

September 21–October 4, 1993: Russian President Boris Yeltsin, aided by the Russian Armed Forces, extralegally dissolves the Supreme Soviet and suspends the constitution in response to impeachment proceedings against him

Sao Tomé and Príncipe

August 15, 1995: Manuel Quintas de Almeida overthrows Miguel Trovoada for six days

July 16, 2003: Fernando Pereira (major) overthrows Fradique de Menezes for seven days

Sierra Leone	April 29, 1992: Valentine Strasser overthrows Joseph Saidu Momoh January 16, 1996: Julius Maada Bio overthrows Valentine Strasser May 25, 1997: Johnny Paul Koroma overthrows Ahmad Tejan Kabbah
Solomon Islands	2000: Coup by the Malaita Eagle Force
Somalia	January 26, 1991: Mohamed Farrah Aidid and the United Somali Congress overthrow Mohamed Siad Barre, beginning the Somali Civil War
Sudan	April 10, 2019: The Sudanese Armed Forces led by Ahmed Awad Ibn Auf overthrow Omar Hassan Ahmad al-Bashir during the Sudanese Revolution
Suriname	December 24, 1990: President Ramsewak Shankar dismissed by Suriname's military
Thailand	February 24, 1991: Sunthorn Kongsompong overthrows Chatichai Choonhavan September 19, 2006: Sonthi Boonyaratglin overthrows Thaksin Shinawatra May 22, 2014; Prayut Chan-o-cha overthrows Niwatthamrong Boonsongpaisan
Tunisia	July 25, 2021: Kais Saied suspended parliament and take all powers on one hand (2021 Tunisian Political Crisis)
Turkey	February 28, 1997: The general staff issues a memorandum demanding the reversal of several policies of the Islamist government of Necmettin Erbakan, precipitating its collapse. Because of the lack of an overt military takeover, the event is popularly known as the "postmodern coup" (Turkish: Post-modern darbe)

April 27, 2007: Amidst a political deadlock concerning ongoing presidential elections, the General Staff issues a statement, later called E-memorandum, about the presidential election understood to be a criticism of the ruling Justice and Development Party's candidate, Abdullah Gul. The crisis was resolved by an early election held later that year, which resulted in Gul's winning the presidency in a landslide.

July 15, 2016: A group within the Turkish military-linked by the Turkish government to the Gulen movement, the Peace at Home Council, made a failed military attempt to overthrow the government of President Recep Tayyip Erdoğan

Trinidad and Tobago
July 27 to August 1, 1990: Failed coup attempt by Islamist Jamaat al Muslimeen organization led by Yasin Abu Bakr against Prime Minister A. N. R. Robinson

United States
2020: Gretchen Whitmer kidnapping plot; The Federal Bureau of Investigation (FBI) uncovered a plot by far-right militia members to kidnap Gretchen Whitmer, the Governor of Michigan, and violently overthrow the state government

January 6, 2021: Supporters of the US President breach the US Capitol in an attempt to prevent the certification of the 2020 election results

Venda
April 5, 1990: Gabriel Ramushwana overthrows Frank Ravele

Venezuela	1992: A pair of failed coup attempts against President Carlos Andrés Pérez led by Hugo Chávez and his group, MBR-200
	2002: Brief coup against Hugo Chávez led by the country's military high command during a confederación de Trabajadores de Venezuela (National Federation of Trade Unions) general strike
Yemen	2014–2015: A semi-successful coup against President Abdrabbuh Mansur Hadi led by the Houthis
	2018: Yemeni coup d'état by the Southern Movement
Zambia	July 1, 1990: Mwamba Luchembe unsuccessfully attempted to overthrow President Kenneth Kaunda
	November 14, 2017: A coup resulted in the removal of longtime President Robert Mugabe

In addition to the 119 coups and coup attempts that are noted above, there have been a few noteworthy examples of anti-government extremist plots and attacks against American leadership and public interests from the 1990s to the present. The terms *nationalist*, *White nationalist*, and *domestic terrorist* have all been used to describe those individuals who target government and public locals and entities on American soil. These actors believe that an act of extreme violence against the governments and public interests of our nation has the potential to force change. For the purposes of this book, I reserve my personal opinions and feelings about any of these actors, as it is of no import, and more, beyond the scope and intent of my stated purposes here.

On April 19, 1995, now infamous domestic terrorist Timothy McVeigh detonated a makeshift fertilizer bomb, which he had concealed inside of a rented U-Haul truck in front of the Alfred P. Hurrah Federal Building in Oklahoma City, Oklahoma, killing 168 people, including 19 children. More than 650 others were injured in the attack. McVeigh's strike was understood to be the deadliest of its kind on American soil until the World Trade Center was attacked on September 11, 2001.

The apparent motivations for McVeigh's heinous attack had been (1) the federal government's raid on the Branch Davidian religious sect near Waco, Texas in 1993 that left seventy-six (76) civilians dead, including women and children; (2) an armed standoff with federal agents in the mountains of Ruby Ridge, Idaho, that left a fourteen-year-old boy, his mother, and a federal agent dead; and (3) his growing anger against the US government, believing that the country was being taken in an intolerable direction, and McVeigh's desire to spark a revolution to reverse its course.

It was learned that McVeigh had chosen April 19, 1995, because that date marked the two-year anniversary of the Waco siege's violent and tragic end. The Federal Justice System put McVeigh to death by lethal injection at a federal prison in Terre Haute, Indiana, on June 11, 2001. McVeigh remained expressionless as he was strapped to the prison deathbed gurney in the execution room where he would soon thereafter take his last breaths.

In an effort to ensure that we never forget what was done on that woebegone day, and all those who were lost, there is a memorial and museum scene which has since been established at the Oklahoma City, Oklahoma, bombing site. Thoughtfully, the gates to the memorial display the times, 9:01 a.m. and 9:03 a.m., with a reflecting pool, which stands between them showing 9:02 a.m., the very minute that the fertilizer bomb exploded. There are metal chairs set up which represent those 168 souls who were lost by McVeigh's merciless assault, and the "Survivor Tree" (an American elm which had withstood the explosion) stands on a small hill and provides shade to the memorial site beneath it.

In 2020, "[T]he FBI and Department of Homeland Security issued a bulletin to law enforcement agencies across the country, highlighting the 'persistent and evolving' threat from violent White supremacists and other domestic terrorists."

The bulletin noted that because of Mcveigh's attack, 1995 was the nation's most lethal year for domestic terrorism attacks. [And that, 2019] was the nation's second most lethal year for domestic terrorism attacks, the bulletin said." (See: FBI Bulletin Story at abcnews.go.com)

In March 2020, after learning of, and being inspired by, the destructive and murderous acts of Timothy McVeigh and the Oklahoma City bombing, which had occurred nearly twenty-five years earlier, thirty-six-year-old Timothy Wilson, a resident of Raymore, Missouri, began solidifying his depraved plan to blow up a Kansas City, Kansas community hospital, which at that time was filled to near capacity with COVID-19 pandemic patients seeking urgent care. However, and only by the grace of God and some great law enforcement work in the case, Timothy Wilson's plans were discovered and foiled by an undercover FBI agent who had been posing as a trusted associate of Wilson's. Although the physical target in this story was not that of a government agency per se, it was Wilson's anti-government views and ideology that were working to motivate his contemptible and destructive intentions.

According to ABC News reports, the FBI has arrested, "[A] few hundred Americans suspected of ties to domestic terrorism or violent White supremacy" from 2017 thru 2020, a current-day social phenomenon that seems to be worsening as our country's cultural and political divides deepen. (See: ABC News headline, "Nation's Deadliest Domestic Terrorist Inspiring New Generation of Hate-Filled 'Monsters,' FBI records show"; story at abcnews.go.com)

In October 2020, Gretchen Whitmer was the Democrat governor of the State of Michigan. She was also the alleged target of an antigovernment domestic terrorist militia group in her state that was reportedly plotting to kidnap her and subject her to a mock trial for crimes, which they charged her with as a result of her statewide restrictive COVID-19 policies and mandates. Upon finding her guilty as charged, which was an apparently foregone conclusion once she was in their custody and even before her so-called trial was held, the group had planned to impose a sentence of death and then execute her.

This group of fourteen men who had allegedly been involved in the plot, notably all White, had made plans to attack other elected state officials in Michigan and thereby trigger an all-out civil war. Their expressed endgame goal was to create a self-sufficient society. However, and prior to the kidnapping plot even being discovered, the group had apparently aroused the attention of the FBI, in March 2020, when information came to light of their alleged plans to also *target* and *kill* police. All fourteen men who were said to be involved have been arrested for crimes against the state by conspiring in both aforementioned plots and are now in custody and working their way through the Federal Government's Criminal Justice System.

On Wednesday, January 6, 2021, tens of thousands of supporters of President Donald J. Trump marched to the United States Capitol Building in Washington D.C., with hundreds forcing entry into the Halls of Congress through windows and doors once they arrived, in an attempt to overthrow the 2020 presidential election results, which they believed were unlawful and *rigged*. That is to say, the Trump supporters were of the belief that there had been deliberate and significant *voter fraud* during the election, and they felt compelled as *nationalist* and *patriots* of this country to use physical force, and if necessary, violence, to prevent the unlawful certification of the Electoral College votes. These supporters had wholeheartedly believed that the Democrats were "stealing the election" from the rightful winner and true president, Trump, and were willing to take part in an insurrection to protect our country and their understanding of true justice and American democracy. It is important to note that many taking part in the assault upon the United States Capitol Building were military, ex-military, law enforcement, and state and city leaders. Consequently, five people died as a result of the insurrection at the Capitol, and hundreds of Trump supporters from that day have been tracked down and arrested by the FBI and assisting law enforcement agencies.

Since the insurrection and the certification of the 270 Electoral College votes on the following day, January 7, 2021, the political divide in America has deepened to a new depth never seen before in recent history, with no near-term political reconciliation in sight and large populations in America refusing to call Joe Biden their president. Donald J. Trump has publically announced his plans to run for president once again in 2024, and his *base* in the Republican Party has rallied around the idea and him once again for that cause.

Looking at just the limited facts and evidence which we have examined above, there is no logical-minded person who would seriously contend with the statement that we are living in a day and age when global anti-government sentiment and hostility are at an all-time high, widespread, and steadily growing at a pace never seen before in recent world history.

The citizen populations of the world seem to no longer have the previously invested faith and trust in those who are charged with establishing and securing their common liberties, welfare, and defense. Stated a different way, the evidence presented above shows that there is a newly manifested social distrust, with increasing animosity, toward our present world government leadership, within the citizenry that is subject to their rule of power and global widespread protests and violence against the same are commonplace and ongoing.

The cause(s) of the global civil unrest is complex, multifaceted, and seemingly expanding with the emergence of each new social, health, economic, and security challenge that arises. Racial injustice issues, government COVID-19 responses and mandates, rising costs of living, and national security issues and threats all have served to help kindle this newly ignited spirit of rebellion within the populations of the world. An undertone of apprehension, uncertainty, and a healthy fear of what may be coming next all have left the populations on edge.

However, and notwithstanding the cause(s) for why the populations of the world are currently unsettled, the clear and undisputable fact is that they are, and this global event of the populations turning against their governments in response, or "kingdom ris[ing] against kingdom," is occurring at the same point in time as the previously discussed last three prophetic *signs*. Ergo, the fourth sign of Jesus's prophecy is fulfilled in light of the foregoing facts and evidence, and we are encouraged to move forward with our examination of the fifth.

KINGDOM AGAINST KINGDOM ☑

CHAPTER 6

Widespread Food Scarcity and Shortages

And there will be famines.

—Matthew 24:7

IN THE MATTHEW 24 prophecy that we are examining here, Jesus predicted that there would be an apparent widespread—or global—*famine* on the earth during the Beginning of Sorrows.

The word *famine* is defined by *the Concise Oxford English Dictionary: 11ᵗʰ Edition Revised © Oxford University Press 2008* as "Extreme scarcity of food; a shortage."

In an effort to solidify our understanding of this unambiguous and straightforward definition of *famine*, let us consider it stated in this way: if food is extremely difficult to find and/or purchase, or if there is a lack of food to go around, that is the very definition of famine.

More often than not, in today's world, terms and phrases such as *acute hunger* conditions, *extreme hunger* conditions, *malnutrition* conditions, *food insecurity* conditions, and *global food crises* conditions are all used by government officials and global food support organizations to describe the struggles of the ever-increasing starving populations of our world. The problem that arises when these spokesmen and spokeswomen use these softer terms and phrases to explain the critical—and worsening—situation of widespread famine is that the seriousness of the situation is intentionally—and wrongly—minimized by them not calling the dire event what it is. Most assuredly the minimization is occurring for the purposes of providing false hope to the global community that the situation can be turned around by collective efforts and thereby stemming off global panic and food hoarding by those of us who are not yet as severely impacted by the global crises. But make no mistake, these terms and phrases that are being used to mislead and conceal themselves serve as proof that such an impacted populace is in the throes of famine.

Moreover, it seems a bit odd to me that we should call a famine by any other name, since by any other name, it is still a famine. To this point, I would submit to you that if a population does not have access to sufficient food intake on a regular and consistent (daily) bases, to stimulate and maintain good physical and mental health, the chief cause of that community's hunger and malnutrition is rightly identified as, and called, a famine (i.e., *scarcity* or *a shortage* of food). My main point here being, regardless of whether or not our world governments and global food support organizations label a food shortage a famine, that is what it is. With this logical assessment and conclusion in mind, let us move forward.

It is important to understand that there are two main types (or categories) of famine, those being one that is caused by an actual shortage of food being grown and/or produced and another that is caused by an inability of consumers in being able to buy the food that is available for sale because of a lack of finances or as a result of some other obstruction to them completing the food purchase, such as *supply-chain* issues. Historically speaking, a population usually faces one type of cause for a famine or the other at any given time; however, in our present global food crises dilemma, which will be discussed at length in the following pages, it would seem that both types of causes for famine are at play.

There are many things that can, and in fact do, contribute to a famine occurring at any given time and location on the earth, which includes, but is not limited to, poor government leadership, labor shortages, social poverty, war, drought, disease, extreme weather events, and natural disasters.

From the outset of the global COVID-19 pandemic in 2019, after government Chinese scientists in Wuhan, China, created COVID-19 and released it into the population, and leading up to our present day, the abovementioned causative factors (reasons) for famine have been present and increasing in severity on the world stage. The advent and rapid spread of COVID-19 has been a direct cause of social poverty and labor shortages in the United States and around the world, by creating situations where people are unable to, or are prevented from, working because of the high transmissibility rate and health risks associated with the virus, and this current man-made pandemic, in conjunction with poor government leadership, new and ongoing wars, severe droughts, extreme weather events, and other natural disasters, are currently plaguing nearly every major continent of our planet. It is those conditions, which are now occurring simultaneously, that have begun to result in widespread famine, and that famine will worsen, globally, in the very short term, as we make our way through this prophetic period and the sorrows which identify its start.

The emergence and spread of famine on the world stage are not lost on those in positions of power, and, notwithstanding their aforementioned intent to conceal its actual severity, action has been taken to mitigate the consequences of the global food crises. In 2016, the United Nations (UN) began generating an annual "Global Report on Food Crises," which documents the severity of the global food crises for that year, explaining the steps in mitigation that have been, and which are being, made to lessen its impact and that predicts conditions moving forward.

Since we are focused on the current world famine, which I have suggested truly began spreading in 2019, I have incorporated the UN's Global Report on Food Crises for the years 2019 thru 2022 below. The data and predictions are relevant to the Matthew 24 prophecy being discussed. In addition, we will review similar reports from the World Food Programme (WFP), U.S. Global Leadership Coalition (USGLC), and two on-point news articles which have taken note of the fast-increasing food shortage woes now gripping our planet. The aforementioned agencies and food organizations are the recognized leading authorities on the topic of global food supply and shortages.

2019 Global report on food crises | United Nations (UN), April 2019

This year's Global Report on Food Crises highlights the plight of millions of people who must fight every day against acute hunger and malnutrition. More than 113 million people across 53 countries experience acute hunger requiring urgent food; nutrition and livelihoods assistance (IPC/CH Phase 3 or above) in 2018.

The worse food crises in 2018, in order of severity, were: Yemen, the Democratic Republic of the Congo, Afghanistan, Ethiopia, the Syrian Arab Republic, the Sudan, South Sudan, and [N]orthern Nigeria. These eight countries accounted for two thirds of the total number of people facing acute food insecurity—amounting to nearly 72 million people.

The figure of 113 million people represents a slight improvement over the number for 2017 presented in last year's report, in which an estimated 124 million people in 51 countries faced acute hunger. Despite the slight decrease; over the past three years, the report has consistently shown that, year on year, more than 100 million people (2016, 2017, and 2018) have faced periods of acute hunger. The modest decrease between 2017 and 2018 is largely attributed to changes in climate shocks.

A number of highly exposed countries did not experience the intensity of climate-related shocks and stressors that they had experienced in 2017 when they variously faced severe drought, flooding, erratic rains, and temperature rises brought on by the El Nino of 2015–'16. These include countries in southern and eastern Africa, the Horn of Africa, Latin America and the Caribbean, and the Asia-Pacific region. An additional 143 million people in a subset of 42 countries were found to be living in stressed conditions on the cusp of acute hunger (ICP/CH Phase 2). They risked slipping into Crises or worse (IPC/CH Phase 3 or above) if faced with shock or stressor. High levels of acute and chronic malnutrition in children living in emergency conditions remained of grave concern.

The immediate drivers of undernutrition include poor dietary intake and disease. Mothers and caregivers often face challenges in providing children with the key micronutrients they need at critical growth periods in food crises. This is reflected in the dismally low number of children consuming a minimum acceptable diet in most of the countries profiled in this report. (Emphases omitted)

(https://www.un.org/press/en/2019/
globalreportonfoodcrises)
* End of report *

2020 GLOBAL REPORT ON FOOD CRISES | UNITED NATIONS (UN)

The 2020 edition of the Global Report on Food Crises describes the scale of acute hunger in the world. It provides an analysis of the drivers that are contributing to food crises across the globe, and examines how the COVID-19 pandemic might contribute to their perpetuation or deterioration.

The number of people battling acute hunger and suffering from malnutrition is on the rise yet again.

In many places, we still lack the ability to collect reliable and timely data to truly know the magnitude and severity of food crises gripping vulnerable populations. And the upheaval that has been set in motion by the COVID-19 pandemic may push even more families and communities into deeper distress.

At this time of immense global challenges, from conflicts to climate shocks to economic instability, we must redouble our efforts to defeat hunger and malnutrition. This is crucial for achieving the Sustainable Development Goals and building a more stable and resilient world.

We have the tools and the know-how. What we need is political will and sustained commitment by leaders and nations. This report should be seen as a call to action and I commend its contents to a wide global audience.

António Guterres
Secretary-General of the United Nations

The Global Report of Food Crises is the result of a joint, consensus-based assessment of acute food insecurity situations around the world by 16 partner organizations.

It is facilitated by the Food Security Information Network, which provides the core coordination and technical support to pillar 1 of the Global Network Against Food Crises.

The report tracks the numbers and locations of acutely food-insecure people most in need of emergency food, nutrition, and livelihood assistance during the peak or worst point in 2019.

The data in this report shows that the number of acutely food-insecure people in need of urgent assistance in the world is rising.

In the four years of the report's existence the number has never been higher. 2016 [-] 108 [million people] in 48 countries were in Crises or worse (IPC/CH phase 3 or above)

In South Sudan and Yemen more than half of the population analysed were in Crises or worse (IPC/CH Phase 3 or above) but high numbers of people in Crises or worse (IPC/CH Phase 3 or above) do not always mean high prevalence.

In 55 food-crises countries 75 [million] children were stunted[;] 17 [million] children suffered from wasting[;] Limited access to nutritionally diverse diets[;] Limited access to clean drinking water and sanitation!;] Limited access to healthcare continued to weaken the health and nutrition status of children living in food crises, with dire consequences for their development and long-term productivity.

Conflict/insecurity was still the main driver of food crises in 2019, but weather extremes were considered the key driver for 26 [million] people in Africa, 4.4. [million] in Central America and 3 [million] in [the] Middle East and Asia.

Economic shocks formed the key driver for 14 [million] in Latin America and the Caribbean and 10 [million] in Africa.

Fifty-two percent, more than half, were hosted in 8 countries of which 4 experienced major food crises.

In mid-2019, there were 44.9 million internally displaced people in the world.

Nine out of 10 countries with the largest numbers of internally displaced people experienced major food crises. Each of these countries had over 1.5 million internally displaced people.

Conflict/insecurity, weather extremes, desert locusts, economic shocks and COVID-19 are expected to be key drivers of acute food insecurity.

The novel coronavirus (COVID-19) is having an unprecedented impact around the world, both in health and socioeconomic terms.

The 55 food-crises countries will likely be highly vulnerable, to the consequences of this pandemic, as will countries that are net food importers, oil exporters and those dependent on tourism and remittances for income.

Given the unprecedented nature of the crises, creating a better understanding of the potential impacts of COVID-19 on food security and related vulnerabilities is critical.

The Global Network against Food Crises will engage to monitor the situation against the data currently available and will strive to provide timely data, analyses and intelligence on the impact of COVID-19 on food security and nutrition.

The global international community must accelerate efforts to tackle hunger[']s root causes during the Decade of Action if it expects a sustainable future for all by 2023.

(https://www.un.org/press/en/2020/
globalreportonfoodcrises)
* End of report *

2021 GLOBAL REPORT ON FOOD CRISES | UNITED NATIONS (UN)

The magnitude and severity of food crises worsened in 2020 as protracted conflict, the economic fallout of COVID-19 and weather extremes exacerbated pre-existing fragilities. Forecasts point to a grim outlook for 2021, with the threat of Famine persisting in some of the world's worst food crises.

By the end of 2020, the global goal of achieving zero hunger by 2030 seemed increasingly out of reach. This follows another annual rise in the numbers of acutely food-insecure people in need of urgent food, nutrition and livelihood assistance.

The GRFC focusses on food crises where the local capacities to respond are insufficient, promoting a request for the urgent mobilization of the international community, as well as countries/territories where data are available based on the Integrated Food Security Phase Classification (IPC) and Cadre Harmonise (CH) or comparable sources.

At least 155 million people in 55 countries/territories were in Crises or worse (IPC/CH Phase 3 or above) in 2020, an increase of around 20 million people from 2019. Among the 39 countries/territories included in the GRFC since 2016, the number of people in Crises or worse (IPC/CH Phase 3 or above) or equivalent has increased from 94 million to 147 million people, reflecting worsening levels and wider geographical coverage.

Around 28 million people across 38 of the 43 countries/ territories with IPC/CH analyses were in Emergency or worse (IPC/CH Phase 4 or above) and required urgent action to save lives and livelihoods. Most people in these dire circumstances were in Afghanistan/ the Democratic Republic of Congo, the Sudan and Yemen/ with at least 2 million people in Emergency (IPC/CH Phase 4) in each country.

In South Sudan, Ethiopia, Haiti and Zimbabwe, more than 1 million people were in Emergency (IPC Phase 4). In six countries, more than 10 percent of the analysed population were in Emergency (IPC Phase 4) (Afghanistan, the Central African Republic, Haiti, South Sudan, Yemen and Zimbabwe). Around 133,000 people were in the most severe phase Catastrophe (IPC/CH Phase 5), in Burkina Faso, South Sudan and Yemen and needed urgent action to prevent widespread death and total collapse of livelihoods.

In South Sudan, the number of people in Catastrophe (IPC Phase 5) rose from zero in May/June 2020 to 92,000 in October/November 2020, and increased further to 105,000 in six countries by December. The IPC Famine Review Committee warned that four western payams of South Sudan's Pibor county faced Famine Likely (IPC Phase 5) in October/December 2020, while two other eastern payams were at Risk of Famine by December 2020 (IPC and external reviews, December 2020). These figures are an indication of the severe impact of protracted crises on livelihoods and nutrition, which can eventually lead to extreme consequences such as destitution and death. The high numbers of people in Emergency (IPC/CH Phase 4) and Catastrophe (IPC/CH Phase 5) highlight an extremely serious situation in which acute malnutrition and mortality are expected to increase significantly among the acutely food-insecure population, should humanitarian intervention fail to reach them and help them meet basic food needs. Repeated adverse events have progressively eroded the capacity of vulnerable households to recover from shocks. An additional 208 million people in 43 countries were classified in Stressed (IPC/CH Phase 2) in this report.

The worse food crises in 2020

Of the 55 food crises identified in 2020, 10 stood out in terms of the number of people in Crises or worse (IPC/CH Phase 3 or above) or equivalent, six of these were in Africa (the Democratic Republic of the Congo, the Sudan, Northern Nigeria, Ethiopia, South Sudan and Zimbabwe), two in the Middle East (the Syrian Arab Republic and Yemen), one in the Americas (Haiti) and one in South Asia (Afghanistan).

For the third consecutive year, three conflict-affected countries, the Democratic Republic of the Congo, Yemen and Afghanistan, had the largest populations in Crises or worse (IPC Phase 3 or above). These three, plus the Syrian Arab Republic, accounted for nearly 40 percent of the total population in these phases.

In terms of prevalence, the Central African Republic, South Sudan and the Syrian Arab Republic had more than half of their analysed populations in Crises or worse (IPC Phase 3 or above) or equivalent. Five countries, Afghanistan, Haiti, Lesotho, Yemen and Zimbabwe, had between 40 and 45 percent of the analysed populations in Crises or worse (IPC Phase 3 or above). Twelve countries saw large increases in absolute terms between 2019 and 2020. The biggest increases in the populations in Crises or worse (IPC/CH Phase 3 or above) or equivalent were in the Democratic Republic of the Congo, northern Nigeria, the Sudan and the Syrian Arab Republic. Other countries that saw a major increase were Afghanistan, Burkina Faso, Burundi, Cameroon, Honduras, Mozambique, Sierra Leone and Uganda.

In 2020, over 15.8 million children under 5 years old living in 55 food crises were suffering from wasting. Nearly half of these (7.2 million) lived in the 10 worst food crises (by number of people in IPC/CH Phase 3 or above).

The situation was particularly concerning in northern Nigeria, Ethiopia, the Democratic Republic of the Congo and the Sudan, which accounted for more than a third of all children affected by wasting in food-crises countries.

The nutrition situation was particularly critical in countries affected by protracted conflict. Of the 10 countries/territories with the highest prevalence of wasting, eight (Yemen, South Sudan, the Sudan, the Niger, Somalia, Chad, northern Nigeria, and Burkina Faso) are affected by protracted conflict. Conflict and insecurity have disrupted the channels of food access and the functioning of basic health and sanitary services, severely affecting the nutritional status of the most vulnerable, especially women and children.

The 10 countries experiencing the worst food crises in 2020 were particularly affected by nutrition and health service disruptions mostly due to COVID-19 restrictions.

In six of the nine countries with data, vitamin A supplementation dropped nationally by at least 25 percent. The drop exceeded 50 percent in Afghanistan, northern Nigeria and the Sudan. In the Syrian Arab Republic and Yemen, the implementation of wasting treatment programmes dropped by 2549 percent.

The perfect storm: the multiple shock effect. The drivers of acute food insecurity are often interlinked and mutually reinforcing. The sharp rise in acutely food-insecure populations partially reflects the increased geographic coverage of several analyses due to growing concerns about acute food insecurity and also accounts for the harsh economic impacts of COVID-19 in urban areas.

However, the increase largely exposes the devastating consequences of conflict/insecurity, which remained the main driver of food crises in 23 countries/territories, where almost 100 million people were in Crises or worse (IPC/CH Phase 3 or above) or equivalent, up from around 77 million in 22 countries/territories in 2019.

The intensifying impacts of economic shocks, including those resulting from the COVID-19 pandemic, triggered the worst global economic crisis since World War II. disproportionally hurting economics in poor countries and exacerbating already fragile conditions, including in countries with ongoing conflicts. Tens of millions of vulnerable people were unable to afford food in sufficient quantity as they suffered severe job and income losses, often coupled with abruptly escalating and sustained high food prices.

In 2020, economic shocks (including those resulting from COVID-19) were considered to be the primary driver of acute food insecurity in 17 countries, accounting for over 40 million people in Crises or worse (IPC/CH Phase 3 or above) or equivalent, relative to eight countries in 2019 with around 24 million people. Intense weather extremes compounded the severity of food crises and accounted for around 16 million people in Crises or worse (IPC/CH Phase 3 or above) or equivalent across 15 countries. In 2020, exceptionally heavy rains and floods wrought havoc on livelihoods in many parts of Africa, the Middle East and South Asia. In Central America (Guatemala, Honduras and Nicaragua), tropical storms, hurricanes and flooding contributed to a precipitous rise in acute food insecurity, affecting areas where households experienced prolonged droughts in preceding years.

The grim outlook for 2021—Food crises are becoming increasingly protracted and the ability to recover from new adverse events is becoming more difficult. Conflict, the COVID-19 pandemic, and large-scale economic crises are expected to extend food-crises situations in 2021, necessitating continuing large-scale humanitarian assistance. Over 142 million people in 40 out of the 55 countries/territories included in this report are forecast to be in Crisis or worse (IPC/CH Phase 3 or above) in 2021. Around 155,000 people will likely face Catastrophe (IPC Phase 5) in two of these countries through mid-2021, with 108,000 in South Sudan and 47,000 in Yemen. No forecasts were available for the 15 remaining countries/territories at the time of publication.

Five of the major food crises are expected to have at least 12 million people in Crises or worse (IPC/CH Phase 3 or above), led by the Democratic Republic of the Congo (27.3 million) and Yemen (16.1 million), followed by Afghanistan (13.2 million), Ethiopia (12.9 million) and northern Nigeria (12.8 million).

The Famine Review Committee warned that four payams of South Sudan[']s Pibor region will continue to face Famine Likely (IPC Phase 5), while two other payams will remain at Risk of Famine through July 2021. Meanwhile, Yemen faces a continued Risk of Famine into 2021. In northern Nigeria, although no population/area is projected to be in Catastrophe/Famine (CH Phase 5), some indicators suggest that a small proportion of the population might face such conditions (less that 10 percent of the population).

In countries facing the most severe outcomes, conflict is expected to continue to be the major driver of food crises. Shifting conflict dynamics, insecurity and armed violence in Afghanistan, the Central African Republic, the Central Sahel (Burkina Faso, Mali and the Niger), the Democratic Republic of the Congo, Ethiopia, northern Nigeria, northern Mozambique, Somalia, South Sudan and the Sudan could lead to intensified violence in 2021. Although information is limited in areas of particular concern, such as Tigray Region in Ethiopia, continued attention, additional data collection, and humanitarian access are essential to implement an informed, coordinated and effective humanitarian response. Although there is some hope for peace negotiations or ceasefires in certain countries in 2021, the recovery of livelihoods from protracted conflict will be a gradual and lengthy process.

The COVID-19 pandemic and related containment measures are expected to continue exacerbating economic crises and acute food insecurity, particularly in fragile economies in parts of Southern and Western Africa, and in Haiti. Even if COVID-19 can be contained in some parts of the world, slow vaccine roll-out in countries with poor health services could prolong restrictions, dimming the prospects for swift economic recovery.

The perennial threat of poor rainfall and adverse weather events is also likely to continue driving acute food insecurity in many countries. Forecasts drier-than-average weather conditions from March/May in Ethiopia, Kenya and Somalia, coupled with the persistent threat of desert locusts infestations, could result in below-average crop and livestock production, reducing agricultural labour income, restricting food and milk consumption, increasing resource-based conflict and driving up cereal prices in the Horn of Africa. In early 2021, dryness prevailed in Iraq and particularly in southern and western Afghanistan, underpinned by the La Nina meteorological phenomenon.

Conflict, insecurity and weather extremes are expected to lead to further increases in the number of forcibly displaced households, both for those fleeing across borders or being displaced within their own country.

Refugees an asylum seekers face precarious conditions marked by limited opportunities for socioeconomic inclusion and lack of access to social safety nets. The worsening economic crisis in Lebanon and ongoing COVID-19 restrictions in host countries will particularly affect Syrian refugees['] livelihoods and food security status in 2021. In Coxs Bazar in Bangladesh, the social impacts of the pandemic and increased competition over livelihoods could further undermine cohesion between refugees and host communities. Continued economic instability, joblessness, violence and acute food insecurity are also expected to fuel the massive outmigration crises from the Bolivarian Republic of Venezuela and Central American countries.

(https://www.un.org/press/en/2021/ globalreportonfoodcrises) * End of report *

2022 UNITED NATIONS SECURITY COUNCIL | UNITED NATIONS (UN) May 19, 2022

LACK OF GRAIN EXPORTS DRIVING GLOBAL HUNGER TO FAMINE, AS WAR IN UKRAINE CONTINUES, SPEAKERS WARN SECURITY COUNCIL

RUSSIAN FEDERATION DELEGATE REFUTES UNITED STATE[']S CLAIM THAT HIS COUNTRY IS HOLDING WORLD HOSTAGE WITH BLOCKADE OF UKRAINE[']S PORTS

A global food crisis, already impacted by the COVID-19 pandemic and climate change, is being driven to famine levels worldwide by the war in Ukraine and the resulting lack of grain exports, more that 75 speakers told the Security Council today in a ministerial-level open debate on conflict and food security.

When war is waged, people go hungry, said Antonio Guterres, Secretary-General of the United Nations, noting that 60 [percent] of the world's undernourished people live in areas affected by conflict. In 2021, most of the 140 million people suffering acute hunger lived in just 10 countries: Afghanistan, Democratic Republic of the Congo, Ethiopia, Haiti, Nigeria, Pakistan, South Sudan, Sudan, Syria and Yemen. When this Council debates conflict, you debate hunger, he stressed. And when you fail to reach consensus, hungry people pay a high price.

He noted that, in April, the World Food Programme (WFP) and its partners distributed food and cash to more than 3 million Ukrainians, also announcing that the Central Emergency Response Fund will release $30 million to meet urgent food security and nutrition needs in Niger, Mali, Chad and Burkina Faso; a drop in the ocean, he pointed out. Around the world, 44 million people in 38 countries are at emergency levels' of hunger, he warned, noting the Russian Federation[']s invasion of its neighbor has effectively ended Ukraine[']s food exports, with price increases of up to 30 [percent] for staple foods threatening people in countries across Africa and the Middle East.

Most important of all, we need to end the war in Ukraine, he stressed, noting Security Council resolution 2417 (2018) specifies that goods and supplies are essential to civilians survival. There is enough food for everyone in the world, he said, but the issue is about distribution. In our world of plenty, I will never accept the death from hunger of a single child, woman or man, he stressed.

Neither should the members of this Council.

David Beasley, Executive Director of the World Food Programme stated: When a nation that is the breadbasket of the world becomes a nation with the longest bread line of the world, we know we have a problem. Even before the Ukraine crisis struck, the world was already facing an unprecedented, perfect storm because of conflict, climate change and the COVID-19 pandemic. Over the course of several years, the number of people marching to starvation has ballooned from 80 million to 323 million, with 49 million at risk of famine in 43 countries, he said.

When a country like Ukraine, which provides food for 400 million people, is out of the market, it creates market volatility, he continued. The United Nations is trying to reach people inside Ukraine, but that does not solve the problem outside that country, he pointed out, stressing the need to get ports running, with 36 countries importing more than 50 [percent] of their grain from that region. Failure to open the ports in the Odessa region is a declaration of war on global food security, he warned, and will result in famines, destabilization and mass migration around the World.

Qu Dongyu, Director-General of the Food and Agriculture Organization (FAO), highlighted that, worldwide, prosperity is being reversed. Agriculture is one of the keys to lasting peace and security, but the last five years have witnessed yet another spike in global levels of acute hunger. Between 2018 and 2021, the number of people in crisis situations who live in countries where conflict was the main driver of acute food insecurity increased by a staggering 88 [percent], to over 139 million.

With Ukraine and the Russian Federation together exporting 30 [percent] of the cereals and 67 [percent] of sunflower oil in the world, he underscored that what happens to one affects us all. He appealed to Member States to continue providing the necessary aid for food insecurity globally and continue to support the contributions of international organizations like FAO, the International Fund for Agricultural Development (IFAD) and WFP, among others.

Sara Menker, Founder and Chief Executive Officer of Gro Intelligence, also briefing the Council, observed that the Russian Federation-Ukraine conflict did not start a food security crisis; it simply added fuel to a fire that was long in the works. Price increases in major food crops have made an additional 400 million people food insecure, a nearly 40 [percent] increase globally in the last five months and equivalent to the number of people that China has taken out of poverty in the last 20 years.

The lack of fertilizer and record-low inventories in cooking oils and grains have already started to unravel decades of global economic progress, she said. While the Russian Federation and Ukraine used to provide nearly a third of the world's wheat exports and are top-five global exporters of corn, she noted all Ukrainian ports remain closed. The international community must coordinate a global response and eschew a to each their own mentality, she emphasized.

In the ensuing debate that stretched into the evening, high-ranking ministers and delegates also sounded that alarm regarding the war in Ukraine and its impact on the worsening global food situation. In particular, speakers warned that countries in Africa, Asia and the Middle East face an increasingly grave situation, highlighting the risk of famine posed by blockaded Ukrainian grain exports that customarily feed millions worldwide.

Shirley Ayorkor Botchwey, Minister for Foreign Affairs of Ghana, noted that, perhaps for the first time since the Second World War, the impact on food security resulting from one conflict is being seen in every country. Welcoming the acknowledgement in Security Council resolution 2417 (2018) of the link between conflict and hunger, she nonetheless stressed that there is still much to be done to integrate peacebuilding objectives into the creation of resilient food systems. While the current global food security crisis predates the Russian Federation[']s invasion of Ukraine, the war has clearly exposed the interconnected nature and fragility of global food systems.

Echoing those concerns, Michael Moussa Adamo, Minister for Foreign Affairs of Gabon, said conflict not only destroys civilian infrastructure, but it also uses hunger as a weapon of war. Agricultural facilities are deliberately targeted and the displaced persons lack access to food. Respect for international humanitarian law and Council resolutions is essential, he stressed, recalling Member States['] obligation to allow unimpeded humanitarian access without politicization. Welcoming the establishment by Secretary-General of the Global Crisis Response Group on Food, Energy and Finance, he urged the Council to deepen its thinking on accountability for crimes of famine, as they are dehumanizing.

Highlighting the situation in South Asia, Shri V. Muraleedharan, Minister of State for External Affairs of India, said the global South has been adversely impacted both by the conflict in Ukraine and the measures put in place in response. He warned against hoarding and speculation in food grain stocks and noted India['] s announcement of new measures on wheat exports. In addition, he cautioned against linking humanitarian and development aid with political progress, which only exacerbate food insecurity in conflict situations.

Bilawal Bhutto Zardari, Minister for Foreign Affairs of Pakistan, noted that 80 [percent] of the world[']s 800 million undernourished people and the 40 million facing famine inhabit countries driven by or emerging from conflict. Even those not directly involved in a conflict pay the price of war; the conflict in Ukraine puts Pakistanis at risk of going hungry, as his country relies heavily on wheat and fertilizer from that region.

Antony J. Blinken, Secretary of State of the United States, recalling WFP and FAO estimates that people affected by food insecurity due to conflict would increase to an estimated 161 million in 2022, noted that the Russian Federation[']s war in Ukraine could add another 40 million people to that total. That country[']s flagrant disregard of resolution 2417 (2018) is just the latest example of a Government using the hunger of civilians to advance its objectives. The food supply for millions of Ukrainians and millions more around [the] world has quite literally been held hostage by the Russian military, he said, noting 20 million tons of grain sit in Ukrainian silos as food prices skyrocket.

However, the representative of the Russian Federation refuted accusations suggesting his country wants to starve everyone to death, adding that threats of a global food crisis did not arise in 2022. Various factors, including speculation on Western food futures markets and unilateral illegal economic sanctions, are not the fault of the Russian Federation. In the context of the active proxy war with the Russian Federation in Ukraine, Western delegations have essentially taken the entire developing world hostage, leading it toward hunger. Only they can change this situation, he said, also disputing the claim that the Russian Federation is blocking agricultural exports from Ukraine.

The representative of Ukraine responded that the full-fledged war by the Russian Federation against his country threatens some 400 million people worldwide who depend on Ukrainian grain exports, which have almost stopped due to blockages of Ukrainian seaports.

The Russian Federation is also seizing Ukrainian grain for its own consumption or to illegally sell it on international markets. He warned that any country that knowingly purchases the stolen grain will be considered complicit in the crime. This is a war of choice by President Vladimir V. Putin, he stressed. Therefore, it will also be his choice if millions of people face starvation—As soon as Moscow is compelled to end the war, the looming threat of hunger will be over.

Also speaking were ministers and representatives of Kenya, Albania, Mexico, Norway, United Arab Emirates, Ireland, United Kingdom, France, Brazil, China, Romania, Canada, Hungary, Luxembourg, Lithuania (also speaking for Estonia and Latvia), Japan, Guatemala, Sweden (also speaking for Denmark, Finland, Iceland and Norway), Croatia, Panama, Bangladesh, Switzerland, Jordan, Uruguay, Thailand, Turkey, Egypt, Morocco, Iran, Liechtenstein, Slovenia, Algeria, Malta, Ecuador, Fiji (also on behalf of the Pacific Islands Forum), Cyprus, Italy, Venezuela, Bulgaria, Qatar, Spain, Dominican Republic (also on behalf of the Group of Friends of Action on Conflict and Hunger), Ethiopia, Belarus, Viet Nam, Belgium, Republic of Korea, South Africa, New Zealand, Myanmar, Chile, Netherlands, Nepal, Peru, Portugal, Poland, Australia, Maldives, Niger, Indonesia, Germany, Mauritius, Namibia and Greece.

The head of the European Union delegation also spoke, as did the representative of the Holy See, in their capacity as observer.

The representatives of India and Pakistan took the floor for a second time.

The meeting began at 11:04 a.m. and ended at 8:03 p.m.

Briefings

ANT[ó]NIO GUTERRES, Secretary-General of the United Nations, noting that 60 [percent] of the world[']s undernourished people live in areas affected by conflict, underscored that when war is waged, people go hungry. In April, the World Food Programme (WFP) and its partners distributed food and cash to more than 3 million Ukrainians. In 2021, most of the 140 million people suffering acute hunger globally lived in 10 countries: Afghanistan, Democratic Republic of the Congo, Ethiopia, Haiti, Nigeria, Pakistan, South Sudan, Sudan, Syria and Yemen, with eight of those countries on the Security Council agenda. When this Council debates conflict, you debate hunger, he pointed out. And when you fail to reach consensus, hungry people pay a high price.

Armed conflict creates hunger, as fighting destroys farms and factories, drives people away from their harvests, causes shortages and drives up prices, he continued. Today, the impact of conflict is amplified by the climate crisis and economic security compounded by the pandemic. Citing the example of Niger, which faces extremist armed groups and cross-border incursions from Nigeria, he noted only 6 [percent] of its population is fully vaccinated against COVID-19. While Niger is ranked last according to the Human Development Index, it is 1 of the 10 countries most vulnerable to the climate crisis.

Against the backdrop, he announced that $30 million will be released from the Central Emergency Response Fund to meet urgent food security and nutrition needs for Niger, Mali, Chad and Burkina Paso, a drop in the ocean, he stressed bringing funding to almost $95 million that has been channelled through the Fund to Sahel since the start of 2022.

He further expressed concern over the food security situation in the Horn of Africa, suffering its longest drought in four decades, with the WFP warning that millions of people in Somalia face famine within months. Around the world, 44 million people in 38 countries are at emergency levels of hunger, known as integrated Food Security Phase Classification Level 4, just one step away from famine, with more than half a million people in Ethiopia, South Sudan, Yemen and Madagascar already in Level 5 catastrophic or famine conditions. Citing the frightening impact of the war in Ukraine on global hunger, he said the Russian Federation[']s invasion of its neighbor has effectively ended Ukraine[']s food exports, with price increases of up to 30 [percent] for staple foods threatening people in countries across Africa and the Middle East.

United Nations humanitarian agencies and their partners helped bring six counties in South Sudan back from the brink of famine and reached 10 million people with food aid in Yemen per month in 2021, he said. However, in East Africa, the cost of food assistance has increased on average 65 [percent] in the past year, and WFP has already been forced to reduce its support to 8 million hungry people in Yemen, he reported, calling for investment in political solutions to end conflicts and prevent new ones. Most important of all, we need to end the war in Ukraine, he stressed. International humanitarian law, reflected in Security Council resolution 2417 (2018) specifies that goods and supplies that are essential to civilians['] survival.

There is enough food for everyone in the world, he emphasized. The issue is distribution, deeply linked to the war in Ukraine. Citing his establishment of the Global Crisis Response Group on Food, Energy and Finance, he said any meaningful solution to global food insecurity must reintegrate Ukraine[']s agricultural production and the food and fertilizer production of the Russian Federation and Belarus into world markets, despite the war. In addition, donors must fund humanitarian appeals in full, he stressed, highlighting that, almost halfway into 2022, global humanitarian response plans are funded at just 8 [percent]. In our world of plenty, I will never accept the death from hunger of a single child, woman or man, he stressed. Neither should the members of this Council.

DAVID BEASLEY, Executive Director of the World Food Programme (WFP), said that, when the Nobel Prize was given to WFP, it was clearly a message to the world that food security is critical to peace and stability around the globe. What we are seeing now is an extraordinary destruction of the values we hold so dear of feeding the poor and helping the needy around the world, he said. Even before the Ukraine crisis struck, the world was already facing an unprecedented, perfect storm because of conflict, climate change and the COVID-19 pandemic. It was thought that the situation couldn[']t get worse than in Ethiopia, then in Afghanistan and now in Ukraine. That[']s on top of the areas the Secretary-General alluded to where famine is knocking on the door, such as the Sahel and the Horn of Africa, he said.

The number of people marching to starvation increased from 80 million to 153 million before COVID-19, he said. Because of the pandemic, the number rose to 276 million, then due to war in Ukraine, it further increased to 323 million. Of that 276 million, 49 million were at risk of famine in 43 countries. Food prices are the number-one problem in 2022, but there will be a food availability problem in 2023, he warned. When a country like Ukraine, which provides food for 400 million people, is out of the market, it creates market volatility. When prices got out of control in 2007 and 2008, riots and protests were seen in more than 40 countries. Now, protests are taking place, including in Sri Lanka, Indonesia, Pakistan and Peru, with destabilizing dynamics in Burkina Faso, Mali and Chad. These are only the signs for more to come.

When a nation that is the breadbasket of the world becomes a nation with the longest bread line of the world, we know we have a problem, he said. The United Nations is trying to reach people inside Ukraine, but that does not solve the problem outside that country, he pointed out, stressing the need to get ports running. He said 36 countries import more than 50 [percent] of grain from this region. Failure to open the ports in the Odessa region is a declaration of war on global food security. It will result in famines, destabilization and mass migration around the world. He said mothers told him that their children have not been fed in two weeks and they must choose between heating oil and cooking oil. When mothers must choose between freezing children to death and starving them to death, something is wrong, he warned, urging the international community to step up its effort and get through the perfect storm, as it was able to do so in the past.

Qu Dongyu, Director-General of the Food and Agriculture Organization (FAO), said that, worldwide, prosperity is being reversed. There is less food security, less health security, less income and greater inequality. Agriculture is one of the keys to lasting peace and security. The last five years has seen yet another spike in global levels of acute hunger. Citing the Global Report of Food Crises, released in 2021, he said approximately 40 million more people experienced acute food insecurity compared to 2020, bringing the total to 193 million people in 53 countries and territories. Further deterioration is projected through 2022, including places with catastrophic food insecurity.

There are famine risks in Yemen, Somalia, South Sudan and Afghanistan. FAO has stepped up its efforts to strengthen agrifood systems, save lives and protect the agricultural livelihoods of the world[']s most vulnerable.

Pointing out that conflict remains the single greatest driver of hunger, he said that, between 2018 and 2021, the number of people in crisis situations who live in countries where conflict was the main driver of acute food insecurity increased by a staggering 88 [percent], to over 139 million. As the world began to recover from COVID-19, the war in Ukraine broke out, disrupting exports and logistics and seriously affected food availability. Ukraine and the Russian Federation together export 30 [percent] of the cereals and 67 [percent] of sunflower in the world. The increase in energy and fertilizer prices is putting the next global harvest at risk. According to the latest scenarios, it could increase chronic undernourishment by an additional 18.8 million people by 2023. We are neighbours on this small planet village, he said. What happens to one affects us all.

Emphasizing the need to prevent the acceleration of acute food insecurity trends in the coming months and years, he urged expansion of food production at the country-level. Agrifood supply chains and value chains must be strengthened with engagement of public and private sector in support of smallholder farmers and households. FAO has been doing just so in Ukraine, Afghanistan and other countries. In 2021, it reached more than 30 million people worldwide with emergency agricultural assistance and resilience-building programmes. It is critical to protect people, agrifood systems and economies against future shocks, he stressed. Moreso, to prevent the impacts of conflict on food insecurity, it is imperative to increase sustainable productivity, strengthen capacities to deliver relevant services and commodities, and provide access to innovative financial tools and digital services. He appealed to Member States to continue providing the necessary aid for food insecurity globally, allocate new resources to sustain agricultural production in challenging contexts, and continue to recognize and support the role of agriculture in food security and peace and the contributions of international organizations like FAO, the International Fund for Agricultural Development (IFAD), WFP and others. The founders wrote: The Food and Agriculture Organization is born out of the need for peace, as well as the need for freedom from want. The two are interdependent. Progress towards freedom from want is essential to lasting peace. Much has changed since then, but one thing remains consistent. The world needs enough foods, good foods and better foods, for all. Investing in agrifood systems is more relevant than ever. Let's work together effectively and coherently.

SARA MENKER, Founder and Chief Executive Officer of Gro Intelligence, said that her company[']s team, from over 40 countries, includes experts in software infrastructure, climate science, agronomy, trading and financial markets, engineering and artificial intelligence who work with large and small companies, financial institutions and Governments. Underscoring that the Russian Federation-Ukraine conflict did not start a food security crisis, she said it simply added fuel to a fire that was long in the works before the COVID-19 pandemic exposed the fragility to supply chains. Gro Intelligence estimates show that price increases in major food crops year to date have made an additional 400 million people food insecure, a nearly 40 [percent] increase globally in the last five months and equivalent to the number of people that China has taken out of poverty in the last 20 years. Countries disproportionately affected are in regions such as North Africa and the Middle East, Horn of Africa and West and Central Asia, she said, adding that current food security challenges will last several years.

The lack of fertilizer, climate disruptions, record low inventories in cooking oils, record low inventories of grain, and logistical bottlenecks have already started to unravel decades of global economic progress, she said. Without substantial, immediate and aggressive coordinated global actions, we stand the risk of allowing extraordinary amounts of both human suffering and economic damage, she added. Global fertilizer prices have nearly tripled year on year and are quadrupled over the past two years because of supply shocks driven by logistical bottlenecks, restrictions on natural gas which impact the ability to produce fertilizer, sanctions and export restrictions amidst the Russian Federation-Ukraine conflict. This risks significant crop-yield reductions in key producing regions, such as Brazil, United States and Western Europe later this year and in 2023, severely impacting global food security and inflation for three to five years. As well, drought conditions for wheat are the worst in over 20 years; even major breadbaskets, such as the United States and Brazil, the world's two largest exporters of agricultural products, are also experiencing extreme droughts.

She also noted that the price of traditionally cheap palm oil has nearly tripled in the last two years, driven by increased biofuel demand, drought in regions that produce alternative cooking oils, such as Brazil and Canada, record import demand from China, and the loss of nearly 75 [percent] of global sunflower oil exports due to the Russian Federation-Ukraine conflict. While official government estimates from around the world put global wheat inventories at 33 [percent] of annual consumption,

Gro Intelligence statistical models show that global wheat inventories are in fact closer to 20 [percent], a level not seen since the financial and commodity crisis of 2007–2008. Similar inventory concerns also apply to corn and other grains. The Russian Federation and Ukraine used to provide nearly a third of the world[']s wheat exports and are both top five global exporters of corn. Combined, they used to export 75 [percent] of global sunflower oil supplies. All Ukrainian ports remain closed, making it impossible to move any of the country[']s harvested grain across borders. Moreover, Russian exports, which also include fertilizer, are limited because of Black Sea maritime hazards.

Calling on those who have the power to change the course of history, she said there are positive solutions and approaches that can be delivered, but they will require quick and coordinated global effort. The international community can coordinate a global response, eschew a to each their own mentality as to food security and climate risk, be willing to have constructive, albeit difficult, conversations, and jointly accept that what should be addressed is less of a food shortage and more of a crisis of prioritization, she said.

Antony J. Blinken, Secretary of State of the United States and Security Council President for May, said that, according to the WFP and FAO, the number of people affected by food insecurity due to conflict rose from 100 million in 2020 to an estimates 161 million in 2022. The World Bank reports that the Russian Federation[']s war in Ukraine could add another 40 million people to that total. Against that backdrop, the United States has announced another $215 million in emergency food assistance, added to $2.3 billion in humanitarian aid since February. The Russian Federation[']s flagrant disregard for Security Council resolution 2417 (2018), which condemns the starvation of civilians as a tool of war, is just the latest example of a Government using the hunger of civilians to advance its objectives. Let's not use diplomatic speak, he stressed: The decision to wage the war is the Kremlins and the Kremlins alone. If the Russian Federation stopped fighting tomorrow, the war would end, while if Ukraine stopped fighting, there would be no more Ukraine. Since 24 February, Russian naval operations have shown the intent to block Ukrainian ports, while on land the military is destroying Ukrainian grain storage, facilities and stealing food supplies.

The food supply for millions of Ukrainians and millions more around [the] world has quite literally been held hostage by the Russian military, which is using food as a weapon to accomplish what its invasion has not, breaking the spirit of the Ukrainian people, he continued. However, Ukrainian farmers are risking their lives, returning to mined fields, wearing bullet-proof vests and helmets as they harvest. Despite this, 20 million tons of grain sit unused in Ukrainian silos as food prices skyrocket worldwide. Sanctions are not blocking Black Sea ports or emptying Ukrainian grain silos, the Russian Federation is, he said, pointing out that sanctions deliberately include carve-outs for Russian Federation exports of food, fertilizer and seeds. He urged the Council to unequivocally call out the Russian Federation for its atrocities in Ukraine and unprovoked war of aggression. Recalling the siege of Leningrad by the Nazis, when an estimated 1 million Russians died, many starving to death including the one-year-old brother of President Vladimir V. Putin, he stressed: It is on us to prevent this history from repeating itself.

SHIRLEY AYORKOR BOTCHWEY, Minister for Foreign Affairs of Ghana, said that, perhaps, for the first time since the Second World War, the impact on food security resulting from one conflict is being seen in every country. We experience together the profound anxiety of a global economy in uncharted waters, buffeted by uncertain headwinds, she added. Against that backdrop, she welcomed the acknowledgement in resolution 2417 (2018) of the link between conflict and hunger. However, there is still much to be done to build resilience in food systems, to enhance global respect for norms relating to populations right to food and to integrate peace-building objectives into the creation of resilient food systems. While the current global food security crisis predates the Russian Federation[']s invasion of Ukraine, the war has clearly exposed the interconnected nature and fragility of global food systems.

The food crisis that millions of the world[']s citizens confront now, especially in Africa, which is the hardest hit, cannot wait until we have a perfect outcome among all States, she stressed. Purposeful actions that support efforts of developing countries are needed, with a focus on building resilience in economies and food systems. To this end, the scale and effectiveness of efforts by the International Monetary Fund (IMF) and the World Bank in filling the financial gap in Africa in response to COVID-19 through fast-track facilities, contingency emergency financing and the Funds issue of special drawing rights provide a model for addressing short-term shortages and building resilience. Further, she underscored that action is also required by the parties to the conflict to facilitate the movement of food and fertilizer through Black Sea ports and other transportation lanes.

RAYCHELLE OMAMO, Cabinet Secretary for Foreign Affairs of Kenya, said that, in the Horn of Africa, extreme drought could cause up to 20 million people to go hungry in 2022 and make sustaining peace more difficult. Citing similar links between food shortages and instability in Yemen, Afghanistan and the Sahel region, she said the war in Ukraine is now claiming victims around the world as food prices soar. In that connection, she welcomed the formation of the Global Crisis Response Group on Food, Energy and Finance and called for more than short-term actions in the hope of a return to the status quo. Bold solutions are needed to tackle the food crisis, she said, citing the increasingly certain projection that Africa[']s population will reach 2.5 billion by 2050. In that context, she called for a shift in the continent's place in the global trading system, from a source of raw materials to a place of modern agricultural systems with more access to cash and investments, as well as debt restructuring and efforts to build bridges among humanitarian assistance, development and peacebuilding. She also urged the international community to unite in upholding values of market openness with the understanding that food security is a transnational problem.

Michael Moussa Adamo, Minister for Foreign Affairs of Gabon, recalled that, through resolution 2417 (2018), the Security Council recognized the link between conflict and food insecurity. Countries in conflict are six times more at risk of famine. Conflict not only destroys civilian infrastructure that are necessary to produce and transport, food, it uses hunger as a weapon of war. Agricultural facilities are deliberately targeted, and the displaced persons lack access to food. The COVID-19 pandemic aggravated the existing challenges, including hunger. Greater involvement of the international community [is] essential to ending hunger. Respect for international humanitarian law and Council resolutions is essential, he stressed, recalling Member State[']s obligation to allow unimpeded humanitarian access without politicization. Welcoming the establishment of the Global Crisis Response Group on Food, Energy and Finance, he reiterated his support for the Secretary-General appeal for global ceasefire and condemnation of attacks on civilian infrastructure. He also urged the

Council to deepen its thinking on accountability for crimes of famine, as they are dehumanizing.

OLTA EHAKA, Minister for Foreign Affairs of Albania, said that it is undeniable that conflict is now the main driver of hunger and food insecurity, noting that the destruction of civilian infrastructure drastically reduces population's ability to produce food or earn income. Noting that close to 193 million people are acutely food insecure and in need of urgent assistance across 53 countries, she pointed out that millions do not know when their next meal will come. The Russian Federation[']s aggression against Ukraine is further exacerbating already acute global food insecurity, and the blockade and destruction of critical Black Sea ports and other infrastructure is disrupting the critical supply of food commodities and agricultural inputs. There is food in Ukraine, but it cannot get out of the country, she said.

She went on to say that the war in Ukraine could push up to 40 million more people into poverty and hunger, this is the sad reality and she stressed that the Council should play a more active role in considering and addressing conflict-induced hunger. Humanitarian action and respect for international humanitarian law can only mitigate the effects of conflict on food systems, and therefore, political solutions to end conflicts are urgently needed. She also underscored that tackling global food insecurity requires urgent multilateral action in several key areas, including addressing the causes of food and nutrition crisis, reducing the risk of further conflict and investing in sustainable food systems. Further, she supported the creation of a United Nations Special

Envoy or focal point for the implementation of resolution 2417 (2018).

Victor Manuel Villalobos Arambula, Minister of Agriculture and Rural Development of Mexico, said that, in Latin America and the Caribbean, the most serious food security crisis is in Haiti, where half of the population requires food assistance, and more than 1 million people are living in extreme poverty. As an armed conflict in one place sooner or later will disrupt the entire food system, it is important to design alternatives that do not endanger food security globally, he said, noting that the Security Council has the tools to address those challenges. Recalling that resolution 2417 (2018) was an important step in recognizing the causal links between armed conflict and famine, he called for compliance with the provisions of relevant resolutions that have been adopted. Underscoring the importance of early warning mechanisms available to the United Nations system, he said humanitarian and development agencies must be able to identify and prevent situations that could lead to famine and the impact it could have on peace and international security. As well, exceptions should be made on humanitarian grounds to facilitate the work of those agencies in those circumstances. To end food insecurity in conflict situations, resources and priorities must be redirected to humanitarian action and addressing the underlying causes of conflicts, instead of increasing spending on weapons.

Anne Beathe Tvinnereim, Minister of International Development of Norway, underscored that the Russian Federation[']s invasion of Ukraine exacerbated an already strained global food security situation, causing the steep rise in global food prices and food insecurity. Meanwhile, those issues have the potential to spark unrest and conflicts, she said, underlining the Security Council[']s preventive role to play, in line with resolution 2417 (2018). Recalling the recommendations jointly presented by FAO and WFP on food crises in countries with conflict situations, she noted that the acute global food insecurity situation is expected to deteriorate further. In that regard, she called on States to scale up investments in food production and resilience, both in and outside conflict zones. She also highlighted the role of small-scale food producers as the backbone of food systems and of women and girls as food producers, traders, consumers, decision-makers and negotiators. Protecting women and girls from violence, including sexual and gender-based violence, is crucial to eliminating hunger, she said. She further noted that the war in Ukraine has also raised the spectre of mass starvation on Africa, which depends on food imports to feed itself.

LANA ZAKI NUSSEIBEH (United Arab Emirates), noted her country imports 90 [percent] of its food, calling on the Council and the international community to act with urgency and at scale to relieve the food crisis. From Cairo to Cape Town, Africa is facing an acute shortage of food, which will undermine stability and security. She cited a WFP report stating that before the conflict in Ukraine, 276 million people were already in the grip of extreme hunger globally, with that number projected to reach 323 million in 2022. According to the United Nations['] Children[']s Fund (UNICEF), 13.6

million children worldwide under the age of five suffer from severe malnutrition, resulting in 1 in 5 deaths, a morally unfathomable situation juxtaposed against $430 trillion of global wealth. Food insecurity is a root cause and accelerator of conflict, she stated, calling for full respect of international humanitarian law. Sanctions must include necessary exceptions for food and agricultural products, she stressed, also calling on the Council to follow up on risk mitigation strategies regarding climate change. She noted that the United Nations['] Development Programme (UNDP) reports that, on average, highly fragile countries receive a mere $2 per person of climate finance. The level of food insecurity and likelihood of growing needs is a flashing alarm signal, she warned, and the response must be commensurate with the magnitude of the global threat.

SHRI V. MURALEEDHARAN, Minister of State for External Affairs of India, said the global South has been adversely impacted both by the conflict in Ukraine and the measures put in place in response. Warning of repercussions if it does not give way to dialogue immediately, he said the collapse of economies and law and order already seen in some countries will only get worse. The challenges emanating from Ukraine require creative solutions, as shortages can only be addressed by going beyond constraints that bind us presently. In that context, he welcomed Secretary-General[']s call for exempting purchases of food by WFP from food export restrictions, with immediate effect. Energy security is an equally serious concern, and must be addressed through greater sensitivity to other countries energy mix and import requirements, as well as by mutual cooperative efforts. He warned against hoarding and speculation in food grain stocks and noted India[']s announcement of new measures on wheat exports, which will allow the country to truly respond to those most in need. In addition, he cautioned against linking humanitarian and development aid with political progress, which will only exacerbate food insecurity in conflict situations.

Colm Brophy, Minister of State for Overseas Development and the Diaspora of Ireland, said his country speaks to both conflict and food security from its own lived experiences. It is unconscionable, that in our world of plenty, millions are on the brink of starvation, he said, emphasizing that conflict is now the biggest driver of hunger, and by failing to act, the Council has a responsibility to bear. Sounding alarm over the situations in Somalia, northern Ethiopia, Mali, Haiti, South Sudan and Afghanistan, he said the illegal, unjustified invasion of Ukraine by the Russian Federation has caused immeasurable suffering with worldwide impacts on food security. Our response, too often is to address the symptoms, not the disease, he said.

Humanitarian aid is provided to those trapped in conflicts, while the global community lacks the will or commitment to end them. Stressing that war is not inevitable, he said the Council must match its actions to the severity of the situation, which is deepening on our watch, and commit to doing things differently. "Just how many red flags and alarm bells are needed?" he asked, calling for early action to reverse the frightening trends of conflict-induced food insecurity and famine.

Barbara Woodward (United Kingdom) said Yemen is facing catastrophic levels of food insecurity for the fifth consecutive year. Refugees across the Sahel are suffering from increased violence and reduced humanitarian access.

In Ethiopia and Somalia, people are grappling with the worst drought in 40 years. The Russian Federation ignored this suffering in choosing to invade Ukraine, the breadbasket of the world. And now, the world[']s food supply chain is being throttled by the Russian Federation. Across the world, 2 million hungry children, who were already subsisting on a knife-edge, face starvation this year. The United Kingdom fully supports the United States–led Roadmap for Global Food Security and the Global Alliance launched under Germany[']s Group of Seven presidency. The international community must enable the free movement of food. All WTO members must enable the free movement of food. All WTO members must prohibit export restrictions. It is also vital to strengthen global resilience to prevent future famine risks. The United Kingdom will continue to pursue accountability of those using starvation as a weapon of war. The Russian Federation must end. the conflict and the global shocks it is inflicting on the world[']s poorest, she said.

Vassily A. Nebenzia (Russian Federation) said accusations suggesting that his country wants to starve everyone to death are false, pointing out that threats of a global food crisis did not arise this year. As Secretary-General Rebecca Grynspan of the United Nations Conference on Trade and Development (UNCTAD) pointed out recently, the problem relates to food distribution systems and not to a shortage of food products. Factors, including speculation on Western food futures markets, adverse weather conditions and unilateral illegal economic sanctions, are not the fault of the Russian Federation, but have laid the foundation for the current situation in agricultural markets, although Western delegations will not mention them almost at all. In the context of the active "proxy war" with the Russian Federation in Ukraine, Western delegations have essentially taken hostage the whole of the developing world leading it towards hunger, he said, adding that only they can change this situation.

He went on to dispute the claim that the Russian Federation is blocking agricultural exports from Ukraine, emphasizing that Russian armed forces tried opening a humanitarian corridor daily to provide a safe passage of vessels from Ukraine's territorial waters. Kyiv, on the other hand, is worming out of working with representatives of foreign vessel owners in resolving the issue. In addition, although the deliveries of agricultural production and fertilizers from the Russian Federation and Belarus could play a positive role, the illegal unilateral coercive measures applied both countries are damaging the agricultural sector. Nonetheless, his country will have a record wheat harvest and from 1 August until the end of the year can offer to export 25 million tons of grain through the port in Novorossiysk. As well, from June to December, the potential exports of fertilizers will be at least 22 million tons. Addressing David Beasley of the World Food Programme, he asked if there had been any humanitarian shipments of Ukrainian grain through WFP since February, noting that his delegation has reason to believe that grain is not going to the hungry of the global South, but being stored in European countries, as payment by Ukraine for the weapons the West supplies.

Nicolas de Rivière (France) said 2022 will mark a new low in the food insecurity crisis, with the Sahel and Lake Chad, South Sudan, Horn of Africa, Yemen, Syria and Afghanistan on the front lines. However, the Russian Federation['] s war against Ukraine is also a war against global food security, he stressed. While Moscow states that sanctions are destabilizing the world[']s food security, he noted there are no sanctions on the food sector. Let's be clear: Russia alone is responsible, he said. The unjustified and unjustifiable war waged by the Russian Federation prevents Ukraine from exporting its agricultural products, destabilizing global supply chains and driving higher prices. He called for the immediate cessation of Russian Federation hostilities and the withdrawal of Russian troops from Ukrainian territory, with exports resuming from that country[']s ports. France, as President of the Council of the European Union, launched the Food and Agriculture Resilience Mission, or FARM, initiative, endorsed by the European Council, aiming to regulate agricultural markets, guarantee supply to the most vulnerable countries and accelerate the transition towards sustainable food systems, particularly in Africa. He noted that France continues to increase its financial contribution to food aid, which will reach £114 million in 2022, and increase of 241 [percent] since 2018.

Ronaldo Costa Filho (Brazil) pointed out that the conflict in Ukraine exacerbated the international food supply and production chains, which were already stressed to a breaking point by the pandemic. However, unilateral economic measures have a secondary impact on the operation of markets through sanctions on the finance and transport aspects of agricultural trade. Citing WFP and FAO, he emphasized that food insecurity is not a by-product of food scarcity, but rather of lack of affordability and access. Countries must also refrain from the unnecessary accumulation of food stocks, avoid trade-restrictive barriers, and abstain from imposing unilateral measures which may endanger a country['] s capacity to participate in free international agricultural markets. There should be a truly universal, rules-based, open, non-discriminatory and equitable trade system in the longer-term. On the humanitarian front, emergency food aid cannot be a permanent solution. At some point, countries affected by conflicts will need to return to international markets and organize their food systems and supply chains in order to avoid the repetition of the hunger-conflict cycle. However, to do that, they will need adequate and targeted financing to bring their national supply back to order, as well as capacity-building and technology transfers, he said, highlighting Brazil's long-standing partnership with WFP and FAO to promote trilateral South-South cooperation, including in countries affected by conflict.

ZHANG JUN (China) stressed that food security is a top priority and a long-standing challenge facing the international community. The COVID-19 pandemic, extreme weather events, economic recession and geopolitical conflict led to sharp rises in prices, further exacerbating imbalance between supply and demand. As a result, developing countries were hit harder. It is imperative to strengthen coordination to stabilize the global food market. The international community must work together to address supply shortages, including by restoring the flow of foodstuffs and fertilizers from Ukraine, Russian Federation and Belarus, he said, rejecting attempts to weaponize economic interdependence. He thus called for speedy removal of restrictions on food production and trade caused by unilateral measures. It is important to scale up emergency assistance as food insecurity is getting worse this year. When people don[']t have enough to eat, social and security problems will arise, he said, with social unrest already seen in some countries. He called for a deep transformation of the global food system by addressing existing structural problems, such as a concentration of production in certain countries. To withstand risks, it is vital to help developing countries to become self-sufficient. He rejected hegemony and power politics and called for true multilateralism.

Bilawal Bhutto Zardari, Minister for Foreign Affairs of Pakistan, said that the COVID-19 pandemic, economic recession, rapidly rising prices and the escalating impacts of climate change have reversed global growth, and for the first time in 30 years, increased poverty and hunger. Meanwhile, with rising great Power rivalries, political dialogue has frequently frozen, and often, the Security Council has been paralysed. Eighty [percent] of the world[']s 800 million undernourished people and the 40 million facing famine inhabit countries driven by or emerging from conflict. Even those not directly involved in a conflict pay the price of war; the conflict in

Ukraine puts Pakistanis at risk of going hungry, as his country relies heavily on wheat and fertilizer from that region. Spotlighting the suffering of people in occupied territories in Palestine and Indian-Occupied Jammu and Kashmir, he emphasized that Kashmir has become a symbol of the Organizations and Council[']s dysfunction. Action in 2019 and 2022 by India were an insult to the people of Kashmir, United Nations['] and the Council[']s resolutions, as well as the fourth Geneva Convention. Resolve the Kashmir dispute, he stated, and watch how the farmers of Pakistan and India feed the world.

The world is still experiencing a deadly pandemic where millions have died; continents are sinking and the planet is under threat, he continued. "Is this not the time to rise above the conflicts of man and face the threats to humanity?" he asked. Noting that Pakistan has seen the cost of war up close, he added: We are exhausted by conflict—After decades of conflict, ultimately, dialogue and diplomacy were the path to a conclusion. He urged countries in conflict to deploy dialogue and diplomacy in pursuit of peace before and not after the next great war. The international community must save another generation of humanity from the misery of conflict. We can be the generation that ends hunger. We can be the generation that saves this planet. We can be the generation that breaks the cycle. If you let us, he stated.

BOGDAN LUCIAN AURESCU, Minister for Foreign Affairs of Romania, said today[']s debate is timely amid the dire circumstances generated by the Russian Federation[']s brutal, unjustified and unprovoked illegal military aggression against Ukraine. Pointing out that Romania is the North Atlantic Treaty Organization (NATO) and European Union member State sharing the largest border with Ukraine, he said it has been on the front lines of responding to the humanitarian crisis caused by the invasion. More than 1 million refugees have crossed the Ukrainian-Romanian border, where a humanitarian hub has been operating since March. Romania also recently answered WFP[']s call to establish a presence in the country to facilitate emergency aid to Ukraine. Noting the global and multi-dimensional impacts of the crisis, he outlined Romanian efforts to facilitate the transit of grains, seeds and other food staples across the Danube River and the Black Sea, while also highlighting the importance of food systems for progress on climate, development, finance and other global priorities.

MÉLANIE JOLY, Minister for Foreign Affairs of Canada, noted that the Ukraine conflict has been the greatest shock to the already fragile global food system in the past 12 years. In attacking one of the breadbaskets of the world, and seeking to cut off Ukraine[']s economy, Russia is destroying Ukraine[']s capacity to supply the world with food, she said. Such reckless actions are leading directly to skyrocketing commodity prices and inflation. Impressed by the ongoing efforts to create a humanitarian sea corridor for food, she noted that her country is ready to help in making sure Ukrainian grain gets out of Ukraine to those who rely on it. Conflict leads to hunger, while underinvestment in agriculture and high food prices can cause political unrest and conflict. In that regard, her country has contributed more than $380 million to emergency food and nutrition assistance and has spent approximately $1 billion per year in gender-responsive humanitarian assistance to address rising global needs since 2020. Calling for long-term solutions that break the vicious cycle of poverty, hunger and conflict, she stressed the need to invest in climate-smart agricultural solutions. The participation of women is essential in breaking the cycle of conflict and food insecurity, she noted.

PTER SZIJJRT, Minister for Foreign Affairs and Trade of Hungary, said that, as Ukraine[']s neighbour, Hungary faces problems stemming from migratory flows of Ukrainians into the country. The food crisis has created a serious shortage on fragile areas of the world that are already experiencing starvation and were the recipients of Ukrainian wheat. Some of these recipient countries also received wheat exports from the Russian Federation. The food crisis will contribute to the growing threat of terror in some of these areas and to sustained migratory flows. The international community needs to make every effort to prevent a food crisis, he said, stressing the need to provide additional food supplies from alternative resources. Yet, there may not be enough resources in the world to meet global needs. A second step would be to help Ukrainian partners build their capacity. Hungary has delivered, for example, 10,000 kilogrammes of corn seeds, potatoes and sunflower seeds to farmers in the Western part of Ukraine. Hungary is also taking into account the enormous increase in food prices and has implemented price caps.

JEAN ASSELBORN, Minister for Foreign and European Affairs of Luxembourg, said the

Russian Federation[']s unprovoked, unjustified aggression against Ukraine has plunged thousands of its citizens into destitution and despair, with blockaded grain exports affecting vulnerable countries in Africa and the Middle East, where harvests are already affected by climate change and economic shocks. It is war that has caused the food crisis, he stressed, not sanctions. He agreed with the Secretary-General that there must be no restrictions on food exports, also applauding his decision to convene a global crisis response group for food, energy and financing to identify solutions. Luxembourg has contributed to efforts by adopting decisive measures to shore up food security and resilience, allocating 20 [percent] of its annual humanitarian budget to WFP, FAO and international Fund for Agricultural Development (IFAD) initiatives. Affirming his Government[']s commitment to supporting the Sahel region, he called for swift collective global action to avoid the world[']s worst food crisis and avert the ensuing sociopolitical and economic upheavals. Hunger should not be manipulated as a weapon of war, neither in Ukraine nor anywhere else, he said.

MANTAS ADOMENAS, Vice-Minister for Foreign Affairs of Lithuania, also speaking for Estonia and Latvia, said the Russian Federation['] s unjust war has caused unimaginable suffering in Ukraine, with people in Mariupol under siege for three months. Pointing out that starving civilians and the unlawful denial of humanitarian access as a method of warfare are prohibited by international humanitarian law and condemned by Council resolution 2417 (2018), he said the Russian Federation, a permanent Council member, behaves as if it was above the law. The effects of the Russian Federation[']s war are reaching beyond Europe. If Moscow does not stop the war, the rise in food insecurity in 2022 and beyond will be catastrophic with far-reaching consequences. Describing the Russian Federation[']s attempt to blame sanctions and detract attention as poor, he underscored that hunger and conflict are interlinked. The Russian Federation is attacking Ukraine[']s agriculture on all fronts, blocking the transport of hundreds of ships filled with wheat in the Black Sea. His country, Latvia and Estonia are among the first to help Ukraine ship wheat through their ports to the world market. He urged the Global Crisis Response Group on Food, Energy and Finance to make effective recommendations in that regard.

KIYOSHI ODAWARA, State Minister for Foreign Affairs of Japan, stressed the importance of realizing a society where no one is left behind, reflecting' the philosophy of human security, which is an important pillar of his country[']s foreign policy. The Russian Federation targeted critical civilian infrastructure, including that for agricultural production and transportation, in clear denial of Council resolutions 2417 (2018) and 2573 (2021). Japan decided to extend a $10 million emergency grant to help ease the food crisis in Yemen and his Government[']s provision of food aid to Sri Lanka will also be decided shortly. It is important to treat Ukrainian grain exports as a humanitarian issue and to create political momentum. Tokyo advocates for the establishment of a humanitarian food corridor which would facilitate such exports, he said. Further, the next months ministerial meeting of the World Trade Organization (WTO) should reach agreement that food procurement by international organizations should not be subject to export restrictions.

Mario Adolfo Scaro Flores, Minister of Foreign Affairs of Guatemala, said that the effects of the Russian Federation[']s aggression on Ukraine are having a devastating impact on the global economy and the already record levels of food insecurity. Voicing his support for the people and Government of Ukraine, he appealed to the Council to uphold international humanitarian law and human rights law, as well as compliance with resolution 2417 (2018). On a national platform, he noted that Guatemala is very vulnerable to climate change and suffered a severe hurricane season, drought and loss of crops during the pandemic. This affected the poverty level and food insecurity and was driving irregular migration. The hunger crisis must be a priority on the international agenda, particularly in emergency and disaster situations. Such efforts should include building resilient communities, while also guaranteeing the global food supply. In addition, the Council should support early warning systems to provide Governments and humanitarian partners timely, reliable, precise and verifiable information in order to mitigate and prevent food crisis in the event of armed conflict. Commending the Secretary-General[']s Global Crisis Response Group, he also said that it is time to implement the volunteer commitments made at the Food System Summit. Citing Guatemala[']s President Alejandro Giammattei Falla, he said his country is committed to promoting international efforts in line with national priorities in fighting malnutrition and hunger.

JENNY OHLSSON, State Secretary for International Development of Sweden, also speaking for Denmark, Finland, Iceland and Norway, recalled resolution 2417 (2018), which condemned the use of starvation as a method of warfare. At that time, 74 million people faced food insecurity or worse. Since then, the number has almost quadrupled, to 275 million, with most living in areas of conflict and with women and children bearing the brunt. If that is not an argument enough for seriously stepping up our efforts, I am not sure what would be, she said. The situation has deteriorated further because of the Russian Federation[']s aggression against Ukraine. The Russian Federation must immediately allow the export of grain stuck in silos in Ukraine; that grain is enough to feed millions. As well, building and sustaining peace improves conditions for small-hold farmers to access land; communities to grow crops and diversify livelihoods; and for investments in sustainable and inclusive food systems enabling agriculture to thrive, instead of being destroyed. The triple food, energy and finance crisis is one which can only be addressed collectively and multilaterally, she stressed, adding we all have a role to play and a responsibility to shoulder.

FRANO MATUIC, State Secretary for Political Affairs of the Ministry for Foreign and European Affairs of Croatia, voiced deep concern over the current state of global food security and malnutrition. The war in Ukraine has added yet another dimension to the crisis, as both Ukraine and Russian Federation are critical to global food systems. The latter[']s aggression had led to a dramatic surge in food, fertilizer and energy prices, with incalculable human consequences felt most notably in societies already exhausted by conflict. In its adoption of resolution 2417 (2018), the Council acknowledged the link between conflict and hunger and its impacts on global peace and security. The resolution was conceived as an instrument to break the vicious cycle between armed conflicts and food insecurity, he said. However, efficient action aimed at conflict prevention and resolution, as well as ensuring accountability for the use of starvation as a method of warfare, are still lacking. He voiced his strong support for the proposed General Assembly resolution on global food insecurity, which will hopefully contribute to better coordination among relevant stakeholders in support of countries affected by the food security crisis.

Marta Elida Gordon, Vice-Minister for Foreign Affairs of Panama, said the Russian Federation[']s invasion of Ukraine is causing massive loss of life, a humanitarian crisis not seen since the Second World War. The conflict has led to a rapid global breakdown in food security due to the importance of both countries in supplying food stocks, affecting supply chains and prices, with consequences hitting the most vulnerable countries and population groups. Armed conflicts do not mitigate food insecurity, she stressed, even more so when parties to the conflict do not respect their obligations towards civilian protection and international humanitarian law. Dialogue and negotiation based on respect for the United Nations Charter remain the only way to restore international peace and security. She expressed support for the World Bank, IMF, WTO and WFP, working in [] coordination to provide food and financial support to step up agricultural production and keep trade open.

Shahriar Alam, State Minister for Foreign Affairs of Bangladesh, said the 2021 report on the status of hunger presents a sobering picture, and the war in Ukraine has made the situation worse. In his country, agriculture accounts for 14 [percent] of gross domestic product (GDP). It has had transformative impacts, generating employment and eradicating poverty. Bangladesh stands ready to share best practices in food security with other countries. He called for increased investment in technology to enhance agricultural productivity through leveraging international cooperation, including South-South and triangular cooperation. Calling for a more efficient and reliable global food system, he stressed the need to eliminate trade restrictions. He also urged Member States to fulfill their climate commitments and also expressed support for the notion of banning starvation as a method of war.

Pascale Christine Baeriswyl (Switzerland) said the changing climate, the Ukraine conflict and skyrocketing food and fuel prices have created a perfect storm. WFP has sounded the alarm and these crises will impact everyone. About 320 million people will need help with food, she said, adding that the most vulnerable people live in areas of armed conflict, which is a main contributor to food insecurity. The international community, including the Council, must act urgently to guarantee humanitarian access to areas of armed conflict.

The international community must speak in one voice on food insecurity. The General Assembly will take action on a resolution next week on the state of food security, which Switzerland has co-sponsored, she noted, also emphasizing the importance of accountability and in bringing the perpetrators of violence to the International Court of Justice in instances in which crimes of famine occur. There is a lack of equality in access to food, she said, stressing the need for political solutions to end hunger and guarantee food access for all people.

Mahmoud Daifallah Hmoud (Jordan) said food insecurity is a major challenge in the Middle East, interlinked with conflict, requiring solutions based on international coordination. The effects of the pandemic have also led to a great increase in food insecurity for countries already facing the challenges of climate change, water shortage, economic crisis and unprecedented migration. The crisis in Jordan has revealed the weakness of supply chains, he noted, with an ensuing increase in the price of wheat and cereals. The World Bank has reported that these crises will have disastrous repercussions if humanitarian aid is not increased, he said. While the Middle East represents 6 [percent] of global population, he noted it is home to 20 [percent] of those facing food insecurity.

However, the agricultural sector in Jordan employs 20 [percent] of its population, representing a sector that can expand with greater investment and better technology.

Suriya Chindawongse (Thailand) said the food crisis and rising agricultural prices are impacting people throughout the world. All this has placed the global goals in the intensive care unit. Girls and women are particularly affected. He said some actions could be taken to alleviate the food crisis, noting that creating sustainability and food regulations are essential to food security. Dependable supply chains are needed to produce adequate agriculture and food products, he said, stressing that food waste should be minimized and alternative foods to provide proteins for people should be developed. Additional international cooperation is necessary, along with practical steps on a regional basis. He looks forward to the Assembly resolution on food security next week. Thailand is committed to the safe, affordable food plan outlined in the Asia-Pacific Economic Cooperation road map.

RAUF DENKTAS (Turkey) noted that Council resolution 2417 (2018) recognized for the first time the links between conflict and food insecurity. In that context, the humanitarian crisis in Syria is as grave as ever, with 14.6 million requiring humanitarian assistance, and the use of starvation as a frequent tactic of war. The United Nations cross-border mechanism has proven to be a life-saving instrument, he stated, but the Council must act to alleviate the suffering of the Syrian people. He further described other catastrophic food crises, including 20 million people in Afghanistan facing extreme food insecurity, conflict driving 17.4 million in Yemen to require food assistance, and 15 million people in the Horn of Africa suffering from severe drought. Turning to Ukraine, he condemned the unjustified illegal act of aggression against a founding member of the United Nations, stressing: This war has to end. Turkey is working to ease the humanitarian situation and facilitating efforts toward a negotiated settlement. However, atrocities in Bucha and Mariupol have complicated that process, with momentum lost, but talks have not completely collapsed. He noted that 45 African countries import one third of their wheat from Ukraine or the Russian Federation. It is crucial to ensure transparency in agricultural commodity flows and combat speculation, with the international community placing global food security at the top of its agenda.

Osama Mahmoud Abdelkhalek Mahmud (Egypt) drew particular attention to the risk of conflict erupting in countries with economic vulnerability and food insecurity. Failure to achieve Sustainable Development Goal 2 on hunger in turn poses a threat to stability. It is imperative to ensure access of food aid to civilians in conflict areas and to avoid famine. The Security Council has a responsibility to protect civilians from conflict, as well as from famine.

The United Nations system must take a proactive approach and enhance its early warning capability, he said, citing a Council resolution requesting the Secretary-General to report early signs of food insecurity leading to instability. His country is among the most densely populated water-scarce countries, he said, urging the international community to address the needs of these countries.

Omar Hilale (Morocco) said international peace and security and eradication of hunger and food insecurity are priorities for the country. Food insecurity has created severe problems in Africa. More than 800 million people suffer every day from chronic malnutrition. The continent needs to import food products and relies on these imports to feed its people. The pandemic and armed conflict have increased food insecurity, which is now accompanied by a hike in food prices, he said, stressing the need to prevent conflicts that may break out from greater food insecurity. Morocco has invested in food production through South-South cooperation and promoted new opportunities for female farmers and young farmers. He called for innovative, inclusive food production partnerships, noting that Morocco has signed 38 agreements and conventions with 18 African countries to promote agriculture. It has also organized a food summit with the United Nations.

(https://www.un.org/press/
en/2022/sc14894.doc.htm)
* End of report *

WORLD FOOD PROGRAMME—UNITED STATES | 2021 POSTING | ON COVID-19 IMPACT | REQUEST FOR ASSISTANCE

The Devastating Toll of COVID-19

The COVID-19 pandemic is driving millions of people into hunger and poverty. Countries are already in the grip of famine and people will starve without food assistance. We need your help to save their lives.

A Pandemic on Top of a Pandemic

New data about the coronavirus is shocking: Its impact on human lives and the global economy more than doubled the number of severely hungry people to 276M. The U.N. World Food Programme is undertaking the biggest response in its history to serve up to 135M of them.

276M people are facing severe hunger due to COVID-19 44 Men, women and children are on the brink of famine 584,000 people are facing famine-like conditions[.]

(https://www.wfpusa.org/
drivers-of-hunger/covid-19)
* End of relevant portion of report *

WORLD FOOD PROGRAMME—ORGANIZATION | 2022 REPORT

A Hunger Catastrophe

Conflict, COVID[-19], the climate crisis, and rising costs have combined in 2022 to create jeopardy for the world's 811 million hungry people.

The world is facing a global hunger crisis of unprecedented proportions in 2022 and we are at a critical crossroads. Either we rise to the challenge of meeting immediate needs at scale, while at the same time supporting programmes that build long-term resilience, or the world will face even bigger problems down the line.

As up to 811 people go to bed hungry every night, the number of those facing acute food insecurity has more than doubled. A total of 50 million people are facing emergency levels of hunger in 45 countries. In just two years, the number of severely food insecure people has increased by more than 200 million from 135 million (in 53 countries before the COVID-19 pandemic) to 345 million in 82 countries.

This seismic hunger crisis has been caused by a deadly combination of four factors.

Conflict is still the biggest driver of hunger, with 60 percent of the world's hungry living in areas afflicted by war and violence. Events unfolding in Ukraine are further proof of how conflict feeds hunger, forcing people out of their homes and wiping out their sources of income.

Climate shocks destroy lives, crops and livelihoods, undermine people's ability to feed themselves, and have displaced 30 million from their homes globally in 2020.

The economic consequences of the COVID-19 pandemic are driving hunger to unprecedented levels.

And, last but not least, the cost of reaching people in need is rising: the price WFP is paying for food is up 44 percent compared to 2019, and additional US$73 million a month (up from US$42 million at the beginning of the year—before the crisis in Ukraine).

The world is facing a global hunger crisis of unprecedented proportions in 2022 and we are at a critical crossroads.

From the Central American Dry Corridor and Haiti, through the Sahel, Central African Republic, South Sudan and then eastwards to the Horn of Africa, Syria, Yemen and all the way to Afghanistan, there is a ring of fire stretching around the world where conflict and climate shocks are driving millions of people to the brink of starvation.

While needs are sky-high, resources have hit rock bottom. The World Food Programme (WFP) requires US$22.2 billion to reach 152 million people in 2022. However, with the global economy reeling from the COVID-19 pandemic, the gap between needs and funding is bigger than ever before.

Unless the necessary resources are made available, lost lives and reversal of hard-earned development gains will be the price to pay.

In countries like Nigeria, South Sudan and Yemen, WFP is already faced with hard decisions, including cutting rations to be able to reach more people. This is tantamount to taking from the hungry to feed the starving.

The consequences of not investing in resilience activities will reverberate across borders. If communities are not empowered to withstand the shocks and stresses they are exposed to, this could result in increased migration and possible destabilization and conflict. Recent history has shown us this: when WFP ran out of funds to feed Syrian refugees in 2015, they had no choice but to leave the camps and seek help elsewhere, causing one of the greatest refugee crises in recent European history.

The time to act is now.

Levels of humanitarian and development assistance must be stepped up to allow WFP to continue its life-saving work in emergencies but also to build the ability of families and communities to feed themselves and break their dependence on humanitarian support.

Evidence shows this approach pays dividends. In just three years to 2021, WFP and local communities turned 272,000 acres of barren fields in the Sahel region of five African countries into productive farmland, changing the lives of over 2.5 million people and contributing to peace and stability. In Bangladesh in 2020, WFP supported 145,000 people with cash and assistance ahead of severe forecast flooding. This empowered them to buy food and medicine, protect critical assets and transport livestock and families to safe places, preventing losses and damages. This cut the emergency response cost by over half.

However, to achieve Zero Hunger, money is not enough.

Only political will can end conflict in places like Yemen, Ethiopia and South Sudan, and without a firm political commitment to contain global warming as stipulated in the Paris Agreement, the main drivers of hunger will continue unabated.

(https://www.wfp.org/hunger-catastrophe)
* End of relevant portion of report *

U.S. Global Leadership Coalition (USGLC) | 2022 Brief COVID—19 Brief: Impact on Food Security

The rapid spread of COVID-19 has demonstrated that no matter how successful America is at fighting the pandemic here at home, we will never stop this threat unless we're also fighting it around the world. In this series of issue briefs, the USGLC takes an in-depth look at the global response and COVID's impacts on vulnerable populations, global development and diplomacy, and the future of U.S. global leadership. [...]

The COVID-19 pandemic increased global food insecurity in almost every country by reducing incomes and disrupting food supply chains[,] conditions worsened worldwide by Russia's unprovoked invasion of Ukraine. This pandemic continues to create devastating effects on global hunger and poverty, especially on the poorest and most vulnerable populations. Today, the number of severely food-insecure people doubled from before the pandemic to 276 million people. By the end of 2022, due to the compounding effects of continued social, political, and economic crises around the world, the World Food Program[me] (WFP) estimates this total to rise to 323 million people.

The UN warns that without immediate humanitarian assistance, over 43 million people in 38 countries across the globe are at risk of falling into famine or famine-like conditions. Ethiopia, Somalia, South Sudan, Afghanistan, and Yemen are at the highest risk of famine.

Since 2019, the number of hungry people in West Africa has quadrupled, reaching its highest levels in decades. This intensifies an already severe food crisis in the region, as farmers have struggled to feed their families due to drought, inflation, COVID-19 border closures, and political instability.

Food insecurity was high in conflict-affected areas even before Russia's invasion of Ukraine. A November 2021 assessment found that 28% of Ukraine's population has experienced moderate or severe levels of food insecurity in the country's eastern region. That number is projected to rise to over 40% in the next three months. The share of the global population not getting sufficient nourishment has increased from 8.4% to 9.9% in one year, threatening the advancement of Sustainable Development Goal 2 (Zero Hunger by 2030). If current trends continue, 660 million people will still be hungry in 2030.

Supply chain disruptions due to COVID-19 and increased consumer demand for food drastically raised food prices across the globe increasing the severity of food insecurity for the 811 million people around the world who go to bed hungry every night. The war in Ukraine has disrupted almost a third of the world's wheat market, worsening a food security crisis already exacerbated by COVID-19. Without immediate assistance, trends will continue, with climate shocks, violent conflict, and global health challenges driving food commodity prices to their highest levels ever.

In March 2022, world food prices surged at the fastest pace ever, jumping nearly 13% to a new record high. Low-income countries that are already struggling to recover from COVID-19 and rely on reasonably priced wheat, vegetable oils, and other food staples will be hit hardest by skyrocketing prices. This is pushing import-dependent countries in the Middle East and Northern Africa to a breaking point.

The cost of minimum monthly food needs is up 351% in Lebanon, 97% in Syria, and 81% in Yemen. Wheat flour and cooking oil is up as much as 47% in the region.

The price of wheat and oil has increased by 300% in Somalia during the Ukraine crisis. As a result, families are forced to turn to cheaper, less nutritious options, contributing to malnutrition and obesity. Today, 6 million Somalis are marching towards starvation, according to World Food Program[me] (WFP) Executive Director David Beasley. Kenya has seen the price of fuel increase for the first time in five months, raising food inflation to nearly 10%. With fertilizer prices projected to increase by 70%, people are worried about how the country will handle dual threats from COVID-19 and inflation. Below-average rain also threatens to reduce crop production by 70%, pushing 3.1 million people into severe levels of hunger. The COVID-19 pandemic exacerbated child hunger and malnutrition. As the pandemic enters its third year, 23 countries have yet to fully reopen schools to their more than 405 million school children. In 2022, COVID-19 disruptions and supply chain challenges may push an additional 9.3 million to 13.5 million children into acute malnutrition.

5.5 million children in East Africa are facing high levels of malnutrition, due to the compounding effects of COVID-19, intense drought, and the Ukraine crisis. Less than 40% of children in the Middle East and Northern Africa have access to the nutritious diets needed to grow properly.

(https://www/usglc.org/coronavirus/global-hunger)
* End of brief *

BBC News Report | By: Matt Murphy | MAY 19, 2022

The UN says around 20 million tonnes of grain are currently stuck in Ukraine from the previous harvest[.] Russia's invasion of Ukraine could soon cause a global food crisis that may last for years, the UN has warned. Some countries could face long-term famines if Ukraine's exports are not restored to pre-war levels, he added.

The conflict has cut off supplies from Ukraine's ports, which once exported vast amounts of cooking oil as well as cereals such as maize and wheat.

This has reduced the global supply and caused the price of alternatives to soar. Global food prices are almost 30% higher than the same time last year, according to the UN.

Speaking in New York on Wednesday, Mr. Guterres said the conflict—combined with the effects of climate change and the pandemic—"threatens to tip tens of millions of people over the edge into food insecurity followed by malnutrition, mass hunger and famine."

"There is enough food in our world now if we act together. But unless we solve this problem today, we face the spectre of global food shortage in the coming months," he added.

He warned that the only effective solution to the crisis was reintegrating Ukraine's food production, as well as fertilizer produced by both Russia and Belarus, back into the global market.

Mr. Guterres also said he was in "intense contact" with Russia and Ukraine, as well as the US and the EU, in an effort to restore food exports to normal levels.

"The complex security, economic and financial implications require goodwill on all sides," he said.

His comments came on the same day the World Bank announced extra funding worth £12bn (£9.7bn) for projects addressing food insecurity.

The move will bring the total amount available for such projects to more than $30bn over the next 15 months.

Russia and Ukraine produce 30% of the world's wheat supply and—prior to the war—Ukraine was seen as the world's bread basket, exporting 4.5 million tonnes of agricultural produce per month through its ports.

But since Russia launched its invasion in February, exports have collapsed and prices have skyrocketed. They climbed even further after India banned wheat exports on Saturday.

The UN says around 20 million tonnes of grain are currently stuck in Ukraine from the previous harvest which, if released, could ease pressure on global markets.

While the number of people facing food insecurity had been growing even before the invasion, German Foreign Minister Annalena Baerbock, accused Moscow of making a difficult situation even worse on Wednesday.

"Russia has launched a grain war, stoking a global food crisis," Berlin's top diplomat said. "It is doing so at a time when millions are already being threatened by hunger, particularly in the Middle East and Africa."

Meanwhile, US Secretary of State Antony Blinken said the world faced the "greatest global food security crisis of our time" which had been exacerbated by what he called Russian President Vladimir Putin's "war of choice."

(www.bbc,com/news.world-europe-61503049)
* End of news report *

CBC World NEWS—Canada | July 9, 2022 | CBC News report

The CBC World News reported on a massive protest in Sri Lanka on Saturday, July 9, 2022, which was held expressly for the purpose of demanding the resignations of that country's President and Prime Minister, as a result of the economic struggles that had resulted in severe shortages of fuel and food. Protesters involved in the uprising stormed the homes of Sri Lanka's President and his Prime Minister, and both leaders ultimately agreed to resign in response to the demonstration. The Prime Minister stated in an interview that followed that, "Today in this country we have a fuel crisis [and] a food shortage."

In a July 10, 2022, news report, the CBC reported that the revolt had taken place as a result of an "economic meltdown [which] set off acute shortages of essential items, leaving people struggling to obtain food, fuel and other necessities. "The World Food Programme (WFP) is scheduled to meet with Sri Lanka's leadership to discuss assistance.

The Sri Lankan protesters declared that they would remain in the homes of the country's heads of state until the leaders leave.

(Note: No website information provided in article(s).)
* End of news report *

As we had previously looked at the beginning of this chapter, and of which the clear definition was given for, *famine* is the scarcity or shortage of food. Jesus prophesied in Matthew 24:7 that in the Beginning of the Sorrows season, there would be famines in various places.

It is important to note that He (Jesus) did not say that the famines would be occurring in every place on earth but rather that famines would be widespread and simultaneously occurring in various geographical locations on the earth. Obviously, the severity of the famines mentioned at the Beginning of Sorrows season would assumably be an unprecedented event that would catch the attention of those of us (Christians and watchers) who are watching for and paying attention to the *signs* and *season* at hand, as is the case in our current global food crisis dilemma.

A fair and commonsense review and deduction of the reports, brief, and news articles, presented above, can only lead to the conclusion that various countries of our would are in the grip of famine now and that our world government's representatives are warning that many more countries in our world are quickly headed in that same direction at an *unprecedented* rate, as a result of the *shocks* and stressors that were identified through their investigations, factors and conditions that continue to worsen the current global food crisis.

Although our world governments leaders are clearly reserved in their official assessment and in calling the global food crisis a famine in most of the impacted countries, they admit that there is scarcity and shortages of food resources in all impacted locations; interestingly, the *Oxford Dictionary*'s very definition of a *famine*. Their approach is obviously publicized and so intentionally measured as to prevent global panic of the earth's citizenry over the ominous and truly dire situation.

Based on the information and evidence presented in this chapter, it is logical to conclude that the *fifth sign*, which Jesus told us would identify the Beginning of Sorrows season, is occurring in our present time, and in conjunction with those other four signs previously discussed before it. Ergo, we are free to move forward with our investigation of the *sixth sign* identified by our Lord—the *pestilence* sign.

FAMINES ☑

CHAPTER 7

Widespread Diseases

And there will be…pestilences[.]

—Matthew 24:7

IN HIS SIXTH sign, Jesus predicted that during the Beginning of Sorrows prophetic season that there would be notable *pestilences* upon the face of the earth. Since the term *pestilence* is not commonly used in our day and age and so that we might be able to reach an informed conclusion as to what Jesus was speaking about in this part of His prophecy, here in verse seven, it is prudent to search out, find, and understand the accurate definition for the word *pestilence.* Moreover, and because Jesus had said that there would be pestilences, which is notably plural, meaning there would be more than one of whatever pestilence is, we need to identify more than one pestilence in our world today, after we locate and ponder its definition, to confirm the fulfilment of this sixth sign.

The word *pestilence* is defined by the *Concise Oxford English Dictionary: 11th Edition Revised © Oxford University Press 2008* as "[A] fatal epidemic disease[.] Moreover, an *epidemic* is defined by that same source of literary authority as "[A] widespread occurrence of an infectious disease in a community at a particular time."

So, in Matthew 24:7, and for the sixth sign of the prophecy, Jesus was telling us that there would be widespread diseases taking place in *various places* at the same time as the false saviors (sign one), wars and rumors of wars (sign two), racial tensions and conflicts (sign three), civil unrest and insurrection (sign four), and food scarcity and shortages (sign five), which we have previously looked at and confirmed in the earlier covered chapters.

Over the last two thousand years or so, since Jesus's Matthew 24:7 prophecy was spoken, our world has certainly seen its share of widespread disease outbreaks which have officially been labelled and classified as epidemics, pandemics, and endemics. There are twenty of them that are noteworthy here, which are:

- SMALLPOX—Killed more than thirty thousand people in Athens, Greece in 430 BC;
- THE PLAGUE OF JUSTINIAN—Lasting two hundred years, killed fifty million people in the Middle East, Asia, and the Mediterranean Basin, and began in AD 541;
- THE GREAT PLAGUE OF LONDON—Killed more than twenty-five million people in Europe, in 1334;
- SMALLPOX—Killed approximately eight million people in Mexico, in 1519;
- SMALLPOX—Killed twenty million Native Americans in Massachusetts, USA, in 1633;
- THE MODERN PLAGUE—Killed over twelve million; China, in 1860;
- SMALLPOX—Killed 270 people; Boston, Massachusetts, in 1901;
- THE GREAT FLU PANDEMIC—Killed approximately fifty million people worldwide; global, 1918–1919;
- POLIO—Infected sixty thousand children and killed more than three thousand; United States, in 1952–1955;
- HUMAN IMMUNODEFICIENCY VIRUS/ACQUIRED IMMUNE DEFICIENCY (HIV/AIDS)—Has killed more than forty million people; global, starting in 1984 and ongoing to present day;
- SEVERE ACUTE RESPIRATORY SYNDROME (SARS)—Infected approximately eight thousand and has killed 774 people; China, 2002–2003;

- H1N1 FLU (SWINE FLU) PANDEMIC—Believed to have killed upwards of 575,000 people; global, in 2009;
- CHOLERA—Killed ten-thousand-plus people; Haiti, in 2010;
- MEASLES—Killed 122,000 people; global, in 2012;
- TYPHOID FEVER—Killed 216,000 people per year; global, ongoing to present day;
- TUBERCULOSIS (TB)—Killed approximately 1.3 million in 2012; global, ongoing to present day;
- EBOLA HEMORRHAGIC FEVER (EBOLA)—Killed more than 11,300 people; West Africa, 2014–2016;
- ZIKA VIRUS—Although not known to be deadly, infected three to four million people; Americas, 2016 and ongoing to present day.
- CORONA VIRUS (COVID-19)—Has infected 555,367,201 people, and resulted in the death of 6,351,083 people worldwide as of the date that I was writing this page; global, 2019 and ongoing to present day.
- MONKEYPOX—Has already infected more than twelve thousand homosexual and bisexual people, globally, with hundreds of new cases being added to that total each day as the testing becomes more accessible. There are presently 1,800 cases in the United States alone; global, May 2022 and ongoing to present day. (Note: UN's World Health Organization is presently contemplating declaring Monkeypox a "global health emergency"; it is currently in sixty-five countries.

The above epidemic/pandemic/endemic information is easily discoverable through the reader's own independent encyclopedia (book) research/investigation, or for ease, an Internet search using the search terms "Epidemics/Pandemics/Endemics throughout World History."

Presently, COVID-19 with its ever-emerging variants, and the now new and fast-spreading monkeypox disease are now center stage for nationally established medical professionals and the World

Health Organization. The pace of transmission and health impacts of these two diseases alone are unprecedented and present a serious threat to the global community as a whole.

In light of the foregoing, it is clear that there has been, in our world's recent past, and, in fact now are, widespread pestilences upon the face of the earth. Therefore, based on the information and evidence presented here, and not to mention any additional evidence which the reader might independently discover and consider during the course of continued investigation, there is sufficient evidence for us to reasonably conclude that the sixth sign of Jesus's prophecy is occurring now and in conjunction with the previous five. For that reason, we are free to move forward with our discussion of the seventh and final sign still at issue—widespread earthquakes.

PESTILENCES ☑

CHAPTER 8

Widespread Earthquakes

There will be…earthquakes in various places.

—Matthew 24:7

IN THE SEVENTH sign of Jesus's Beginning of Sorrows prophecy, our Lord foretold that there would be "earthquakes [occurring] in various places" during this prophetic period and that these would be happening at the same time as the previous six signs which we have already discussed in the earlier Chapters of this book.

The use of the word *various* here in this specific Bible verse also means *different*, and so for the sake of simplicity and clarity, we can say that Jesus is basically telling us that there will be widespread earthquakes occurring in different locations around the world that we could know about at the Beginning of Sorrows prophetic period. It is important to point out that in Jesus's lifetime, and even while He was speaking this prophecy that we are now studying into existence, there were earthquakes already taking place in *various places*. Of course, the whole purpose of this chapter is to investigate that very matter.

In addition to the fact that Jesus had predicted that there would be widespread earthquakes occurring during this prophetic season, I personally believe that He was also hinting to humanity's access to, and use of, modern-day technologies which, once again, allows for Christian investigators and End-Times watchers, like ourselves (as a result of us being a part of the "connected global community" through the use of said technology), to hear about and see the occurrence of such natural disasters taking place all around the world, from a position of safety and security. That is to say, mankind's modern-day and far-reaching communication technologies, which we have previously identified and discussed back in chapter 2 of this book, allows us (that is humanity at large) to be eyewitnesses to the severe violence, devastation, and aftermath of deadly earthquakes, from hundreds or even thousands of miles away.

Indeed, even for me, as a state prisoner serving a term of life without the possibility of parole (LWOP) in California, and being confined within the prison walls and behind electrified fencing at SATF-Corcoran State Prison, if an earthquake of measurable size happened in another city, country, state, or country, at this very moment, I could know about it through the use of my personal television or state-issued GTL tablet (which features nearly one hundred constantly updated electronic newspapers) before the day was finished. This was something that was not even possible for the *free* global civilian populations of our world prior to the 1990s.

According to some scientific geological authorities on the matter, there has been a significant increase in the earth's tectonic plate activity over the last twenty years. Shifting and colliding tectonic plates are believed to be the scientific explanation (cause) for earthquakes. However, for those reasons stated above, I do not believe that Jesus was necessarily speaking about an increase in the frequency of isolated earthquakes during this prophetic season, per se, or He could have just said so. But rather, I believe that He was referring to our modern-day technological advancements and ability, thereby, to detect, record, and disseminate (publicize) the earthquake event information that would be, and now is, taking place in the various locations around the world in our time.

Today, the scientific information and related seismic data for earthquakes are regularly collected through agencies such as the United States Geological Survey (USGS). These scientific observations and conclusions are then globally publicized through the use of our modern-day media technology mediums (i.e., radio, television, computers, and cell phones connected to Internet servers), and it is these technological advancements, which allows for humanity's information sharing that makes the fulfillment of Jesus's prophecy in our lifetime possible; that is, every Christian investigator and watcher can now be true eyewitnesses to earthquakes taking place in *various places* around the world by using modern-day technologies.

To give one last example, as a result of me growing up in rural Arkansas in the 1980s and early 1990s, earthquakes were something that I had never personally seen, felt, or otherwise experienced in my youth; as they do not normally occur in that part of our nation. In fact, it was not until I was transferred to Calipatria State Prison, in Calipatria, California (Southern California), back in 2012, that I had personally experienced my first earthquake as a thirty-seven-year-old man.

I recall that a subsequent local news report on television, which had quickly followed the earthquake, within an hour of it occurring, had indicated that it had been a 5.1 on the Richter scale. I also recall that I had been out on the prison's *exercise yard* at the time that it struck, working out in the *weight pile* and that it scared the daylights out of me, although I had pretended in the moment that I was not concerned by it at all.

There is no other feeling like having the earth move under your feet, but I digress. As a result of modern-day technologies, anyone can now research the earthquake that I am speaking about and confirm that it actually occurred, thus, themselves, becoming a *witness* to the same.

So why is our focused analysis of what Jesus literally meant by this Bible verse critical? Because as I have pointed out supra, there have always been earthquakes taking place throughout the world, even at the very moment that Jesus was speaking the prophecy to His disciples, but what we have not always had was the ability to witness their occurrences from any location in the world as we do today.

In summation of my point, in today's technologically advanced world, earthquakes are closely monitored and recorded, and we have a means of being alerted and informed regarding their epicenter and other relevant details for each one that occurs around the world if we are motivated to seek out the information and to learn about them. Here in America, the United States Geological Survey (USGS) monitors, records, and reports on earthquakes that take place in our country and around the world. Indeed, I submit to my reader that it was our current-day access to this technology and information mediums that Jesus had in mind when He inferred that we would be able to know about earthquakes that would be occurring in *various places* when the Beginning of Sorrows prophetic season was at hand.

Finally, although the Bible does, in other books covering End-Times prophecy, foretell of latter-day earthquakes being severe and unprecedented in nature, Matthew 24:7 notably does not provide that description for the Beginning of Sorrows period. With that said, there have been devastating earthquakes that have killed hundreds of thousands of people within the past thirty-plus years, since 1990.

There are literally thousands upon thousands of small to moderate-size earthquakes, which occur around the world every day, and this was most assuredly true in Jesus's time as well. Once again, the only thing that has truly changed since Jesus spoke the prophecy is our ability to be witnesses to earthquakes through modern-day technologies. With this in mind, I have provided a select list of *severe earthquakes* (i.e., 5.0 or larger on the Richter scale) to share with the reader, from Wikipedia®, of which I submit serves as evidence that proves we are all able to observe the occurrence of "earthquakes in various places" as Jesus said we would at the Beginning of Sorrows period:

DATE:	LOCATION:	MAGNITUDE:	DEATHS:
1990-06-20	Western Iran	7.4	40,000+
1990-07-16	Philippines	7.7	1,621
1991-02-01	Pakistan	6.8	1,200
1991-10-19	India	7.0	2,000
1992-12-12	Indonesia	7.5	2,500
1993-09-30	South India	6.2	9,748
1994-01-17	California	6.7	61
1994-06-06	S.W. Colombia	6.8	1,000

1995-01-16	Japan	6.9	5,502
1995-05-27	Russia	7.5	1,989
1997-02-28	Iran	6.1	1,010
1997-05-10	Iran	7.3	1,567
1998-02-04	Afghanistan	5.9	2,323
1998-07-17	Papua New Guinea	7.0	2,183
1999-01-25	Colombia	6.1	1,185
1999-08-17	Western Turkey	7.6	17,118
2001-01-26	India	7.6	20,085
2001-06-23	Peru	8.4	129
2002-03-25	Afghanistan	6.1	1,000
2003-12-26	Iran	6.6	31,000
2003-05-21	Northern Algeria	6.8	2,266
2004-12-26	Indonesia	9.1	227,898
2005-03-28	Indonesia	8.6	1,313
2005-10-08	India	7.6	86,000
2006-05-26	Indonesia	6.3	5,749
2007-08-15	Peru	5.0	519
2008-05-12	China	7.9	87,587
2009-09-30	Indonesia	7.6	1,115
2010-01-12	Haiti	7.0	316,000
2010-04-13	China	6.9	2,698
2011-03-11	Japan	9.0	20,896
2012-04-11	Indonesia	8.6	10
2012-08-11	Iran	6.4	306
2013-05-24	Russia	8.3	0
2013-09-24	Pakistan	7.7	825
2014-04-01	Chile	8.2	6
2014-08-03	China	6.1	729
2015-04-25	Nepal	7.8	8,964

2015-09-16	Chile	8.3	14
2016-04-16	Ecuador	7.8	673
2016-12-17	Papua New Guinea	7.9	0
2017-09-08	Mexico	8.2	98
2017-11-12	Iran	7.3	630
2018-08-19	Fiji	8.2	0
2018-09-28	Indonesia	7.5	4,340
2019-05-26	Peru	8.0	2
2019-11-26	Albania	6.4	51
2020-01-24	Turkey	6.7	41
2020-01-28	Jamaica	7.7	0
2021-08-14	Haiti	7.2	2,248
2022-06-22	Afghanistan	5.9	1,000

The above-provided earthquake information is available at Wikipedia® by using the search term: "List of 21st-Century Earthquakes." Moreover, the United States Geological Survey (USGS) is one of the world's leading authorities on earthquakes, and it provides an easily accessible website whereat it maintains an updated list of national and global seismic activity event records that can be viewed and downloaded. For the reader, additional information can be found at either of these information mediums, and as always, I encourage the reader to continue with their own research and investigation.

The list of earthquake activity that was incorporated above is admittedly far from being exhaustive, but it does serve our purpose as real evidence to establish that (1) earthquakes that are occurring in our modern times are able to be detected, measured, and recorded; (2) earthquakes are occurring in *various places* in our present day and age; and (3) the information regarding earthquake activity around the globe is made readily available to those of us (Christian investigators and watchers) who are interested in, and searching for, proof of the occurring prophetic signs of the time.

In light of the sign and evidence examined in this chapter, we can definitively conclude that the final sign (the *seventh sign* of Jesus's prophecy) is fulfilled by our ability to confirm that earthquakes are occurring in various places and that believers are able to know and confirm their occurrences. It logically follows that with all seven signs from Jesus's Matthew 24:3–8 prophecy happening now, we are justified in concluding that we have entered into the Beginning of Sorrows prophecy season. We will discuss what this all means for believers and nonbelievers in the next—and final—chapter.

EARTHQUAKES

CHAPTER 9

The Beginning of the End Times

All these are the beginning of sorrows.

—Matthew 24:8

As the reader may have come to realize by this point of our journey together through the pages of this book, the "Beginning of Sorrows" literally means the beginning of the End Times; that is to say, it is the prophetic starting point for the End Times established by God.

In verse 8, and noted above, Jesus summarized that, when all seven signs that He had warned us of are occurring at the same time—and I have proffered that they would need to be happening on a global scale, as each one is now—this *cluster* of simultaneously occurring events marks the "Beginning of Sorrows" or starting point for End-Times prophecies. If both are truly happening now, and I humbly submit to the reader that they are, then we are now peering through the proverbial *open door* of the End Times.

As I had previously stated in the beginning pages of this book, my purpose and intent in writing down the insights and revelations that the Holy Spirit began showing me back in late 2019, is to inform my brothers and sisters in the faith that global events are now occurring (i.e., false saviors, wars and rumors of wars, racial unrest, civil unrest and rebellion, food shortages, diseases, and earthquakes in various places) which, according to Jesus, would signal the start of the prophetic End-Times period. (Matthew 24:33; Luke 21:31). Moreover, I intended to warn nonbelievers to flee to the safety of the cross of Christ, in genuine and humble repentance, before the tragedies that have now begun to come upon the whole earth overtakes them and they are lost for all eternity in their sin and ultimately condemned to Hell.

To be clear, Matthew 24:3–8 represents the Beginning of Sorrows prophetic period. This is where we are at now—at this very moment—in the prophetic timeline, and hence, it is the reason for my focus on the *seven signs* discussed in this book.

However, Matthew 24:9–14 represents the "Tribulation" and "Great Tribulation"—prophetic periods, which are coming hereafter, and that time of God's global wrath and judgment upon the wicked and rebellious will begin in the very near future. (Note: The "Tribulation" is the first three and a half years, and the "Great Tribulation" is the remaining three and a half years—for a total of the seven years of Tribulation that remains uncompleted which had been predetermined by God in Daniel 9:2's End-Times prophecy.) The period of Tribulation and Great Tribulation is the time (seven years in total) when the Antichrist will rule over all peoples and governments of the world and is also the time when God will be pouring out His wrath and punishments on the *left-behind* (unsaved) inhabitants of the earth who rejected and opposed Him and His Christ (Romans 12:19). These targeted individuals will eagerly embrace the Antichrist and His New World Order.

In between the events of Matthew 24:8 and 24:9, there is a moment in the prophetic timeline when the Christian and Messianic Jewish populations of the World will be *caught up* (or *raptured*) to meet Jesus in the air; it is the moment when we will go to be with the Lord and spend the next seven years celebrating the "wedding feast" of the "bridegroom" (Jesus) and "bride" (the church), while simultaneously those who remain on the earth will be going through seven years of what can only be described as "hell on earth."

The rapture of the church (i.e., Christians and Messianic Jews) is foretold to occur after two significant events take place, which are as follows: (1) the "falling away" of mankind from God and His laws and (2) the revealing of the true identity of the Antichrist to the faithful of God (2 Thessalonians 2:3).

In our present day and age, most of the truly devout modern church leadership (i.e., ministers and pastors, myself included among them) agree that we have seen the first event mentioned above play out over the last thirty to forty years. That is to say, there has already been an unprecedented "falling away" of mankind from godly laws, morals, and values. It would seem that the world has not only rejected God, but it has blatantly and outrightly opposed Him. To be sure, wickedness and lawlessness are now commonplace and spreading rapidly in our day and age, as it was in the "days of Noah" (Matthew 24:37), and sexual immoralities and perversities are widespread "as it was also in the days of Lot" (Luke 17:28–30).

Homosexuality, which is a depravity that God Himself has labeled as an abomination, is actually once again in the course of human history, being encouraged by most of our world's governments and its counterfeit religious establishments.

The second event, that being the advent and revealing of the Antichrist, is the last event that needs to take place before we are raptured. To that point, something for a reasonable mind to ponder would be, if we are actually living in the Beginning of Sorrows prophetic time, which would place us now somewhere in the neighborhood of eight to ten years before Jesus's "Second Coming," then it would follow that the Antichrist is alive on the earth today and most assuredly positioning himself in the relevant political arena to rise to world leadership and ultimately total world dominance.

As a quick sidebar to this book's central theme, and to take a rare opportunity to clarify for many something that seems to confuse even some of the most studied Christian scholars, the "rapture" and Jesus's "Second Coming" are two distinctly separate events. That is to say, the "rapture" is when Jesus returns in the clouds and calls us—the church—up to Himself for our trip back to heaven for the seven-year wedding feast of the Lamb, and the "Second Coming" is when He returns to the earth with His saints—us again—to crush the satanic rebellion, judge and condemn the remaining inhabitants of the earth, and thereafter, set up His earthly kingdom.

In light of these aforesaid insights and revelations, we should not only want to make ourselves busy with trying to reveal the

Antichrist's true identity, so that once we learn it, we might caution our brothers and sisters in the faith about him and warn those who are still in the world about the dangers of following after and *worshipping* him once we are gone, but it is actually our responsibility to investigate him for those very reasons. Christians and Messianic Jews are under a clear biblical mandate to be watchers and to warn others in these perilous times that we are in (Matthew 24:45–47). Indeed, if we, as the church of God, fail or refuse to do so, then who will?

As believers, how can we know for certain that we will be raptured, and thereby, avoid the judgment and torment that is about to be unleashed by God upon the earth? The wrath of God that is about to be unleashed upon the earth is condemnation (blame) and vengeance (retribution) for their wickedness and ungodly rebellion. True Christians and Messianic Jews do not rebel in their spirit against God and therefore are not the intended targets of God's wrath (1 Thessalonians 5:9) during the End Times; we are His righteous and redeemed. The Bible tells us in Romans 8:1 that, "There is therefore now no condemnation to those who are in Christ Jesus, who do not walk according to the flesh, but according to the spirit."

Moreover, the word of God ensures that we will be rescued from judgment as a result of our faith in Christ, and in 1 Corinthians 15:40–53, the Bible explains the *mystery* surrounding our pre-Tribulation rescue.

These things being so, for the nonbeliever who will be specifically targeted by God's impending wrath during the last seven years, some may ask, "Is it possible to escape the judgment and torment that is coming upon the whole earth in the Tribulation and Great Tribulation periods?" The short answer is "yes." The Bible tells us that we should "watch" and "pray" that we are "counted worthy to escape all these things that will come to pass and to stand before the Son of Man" (Luke 21:36). Therefore, salvation through Jesus Christ is the nonbeliever's only hope of escape; that is, they must repent and be saved *before* the rapture occurs.

There can be no serious opposition to the conclusion that the exact *seven signs* that Jesus prophesied would occur are now occurring, and Jesus told us in Luke 21:28 that, "Now when these things *begin to happen*, look up and lift up your heads, because your redemption draws near." These things (*the first seven signs*) have begun to happen, and so I echo our Lord's instructions for this time to each one of you reading this book... Look up. Our redemption draws near!

ABOUT THE AUTHOR

JOHNNY PAUL COLLINS is a forty-seven-year-old ordained minister, who holds a bachelor's degree in theology, along with several other degrees, diplomas, and career certifications in criminal law and social and behavioral sciences fields. Mr. Collins is happily married to *the love of his life*, Eileen Marie Collins, and the two share and enjoy a total of seven children and nine grandchildren (both biological and spiritual).

Additionally, Mr. Collins is a California Department of Corrections and Rehabilitations prisoner who is currently serving a sentence of life without the possibility of parole (LWOP) for crimes, which occurred in October 1998. Mr. Collins has maintained that he was wrongly convicted, and he continues to challenge his conviction. He has been incarcerated for nearly twenty-four years, at the completion of this book in July 2022.

In late 2019, Mr. Collins explains that he began receiving Holy Spirit given insight and revelations into global events that were beginning to happen and that were fulfilling what he would soon learn to be Jesus's End-Times prophecies from the book of Matthew and was thereafter compelled to write this book, wherein he shares the insight and revelations given to him.